AF598727

the single parent's devotional

101 REMINDERS *of* GOD'S PURPOSE *and* PROMISES *for* YOUR LIFE

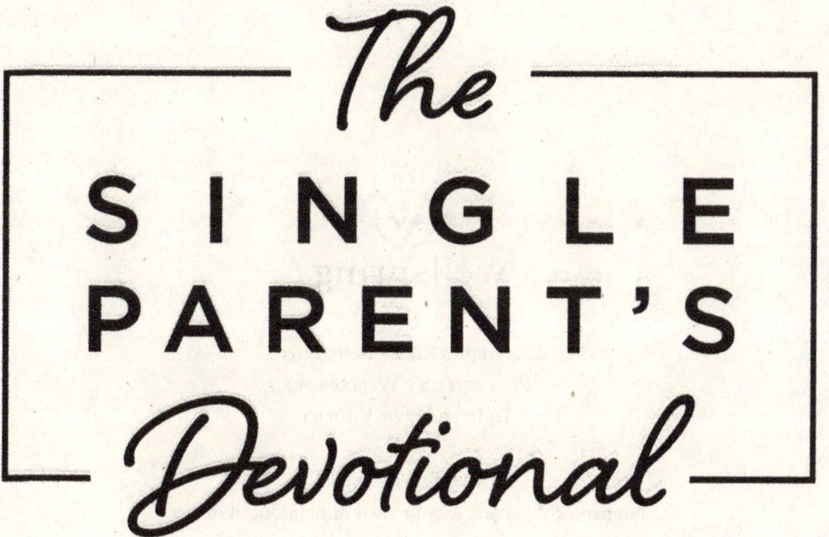

The SINGLE PARENT'S Devotional

KELLY LUGO

Published by Wellspring
An Imprint of Viident

The quotes in this book have been drawn from dozens of sources. They are assumed to be accurate as quoted in their previously published forms. Although every effort has been made to verify the quotes and sources, the Publisher cannot guarantee their perfect accuracy.

ISBN: 978-1-63582-568-8 (softcover)
ISBN: 978-1-63582-569-5 (eBook)

Design by Todd Detering

10 9 8 7 6 5 4 3 2 1

Printed in the United States of America

for Josh & Isabel

Thank you for making this journey with me and for your grace and patience along the way as we navigate this experience together. Your resilience and hope are inspiring, and your laughter will forever be my favorite sound.

Watching you develop your own close relationship with the Lord is beautiful and brings me such peace. I pray you will continue to stay close to Him and live your faith boldly.

God has big plans for you!

It's the greatest blessing and joy of my life to be your mom. And I love, love, love you, all of the time, no matter what.

"We know that *all things* work for good for those who love God, who are called according to his purpose."
ROMANS 8:28

and for all single parents

God sees you, knows you, and loves you.
You are not alone, and you are not forgotten.

"For I am the LORD, your God, who grasp your right hand; It is I who say to you, 'Do not fear, I will help you.'"
ISAIAH 41:13

introduction

This book is about PROMISES.

Life as a single parent can feel profoundly heartbreaking, lonely, exhausting, and unsettling at times, but you're not meant to face all of this alone. It's tempting to believe God's promises don't apply to you and your children, but that couldn't be further from the truth.

God has not left your side, not even for a moment and not even on your hardest days. He is with you, and His promises of protection, peace, providence, and purpose are for you and for your children.

Whether you're a new single parent or you've been in this role for years, I want to tell you that what you do for your family is incredible. I know because I've been a single parent for more than fifteen years. And I know that, as much as you love your children, being a single parent can leave you longing for more—more time, more support, and more sleep, just to name a few.

What are you longing for?

- Comfort for your heart and mind?
- Wisdom to help you to overcome struggles and temptations?
- Practical tips for making this solo parenting adventure more manageable?
- Inspiration to show up as your best self for your children?
- Healing and renewed hope for your soul?

Whether you need one or all of these gifts right now, there's a reason why God put this book in your hands. He longs for you to invite Him deeper into this parenting journey with you so He can lighten your load, guide the way, and make you feel whole again.

As you read and reflect on God's promises for your life, I pray that you will hear God whispering to you over and over, "You are never alone. You are not forgotten. And you are forever LOVED."

St. Francis of Assisi once said: "Start by doing what's necessary; then do what's possible; and suddenly you are doing the impossible." When you became a single parent, you undoubtedly had to shift from doing what was necessary to doing the seemingly impossible as you learned to juggle the demands of work, home, and kids all by yourself. Along the way, you've probably wondered (more than once) if you have what it takes to get through this challenging season.

My friend, as hard as it might be to believe at this moment, you *are* going to make it through this seemingly impossible task of raising your children on your own. You can be sure of it because God will not abandon you to carry this cross alone. This is just one of God's many promises for you.

"The LORD says to you: Do not fear or be dismayed. . .for the battle is not yours but God's" (2 Chronicles 20:15).

I don't pretend to have all the answers, but I do know that parenting in partnership with the Father, Son, and Holy Spirit is how you will not only survive but *thrive* in this chapter of your life. I am certain that God has big things planned for you *because* of your journey as a single parent, not in spite of it.

With Him, the best is yet to come. That's a promise.

—Kelly Lugo

1 heartbreak and healing

"The LORD rebuilds Jerusalem, and gathers the dispersed of Israel, healing the brokenhearted, and binding up their wounds."

— PSALM 147:2

The journey of a single parent almost always begins with a broken heart. Maybe the other parent passed away. Maybe the other parent cheated or chose not to stay. Maybe the situation was so bad you had no choice but to walk away. Maybe you made a decision that changed your life forever. Whatever the case may be, however you got here, you likely experienced heartbreak to the depths of your soul. I know I did.

I was heartbroken over the loss of my marriage, and I was heartbroken for my children to grow up without the security and benefit of a two-parent home. It felt like my heart had been ripped out, and the wound might never heal. But God knew better. He is the Healer of broken hearts, and He healed mine.

The dull ache remains, as I will always wish my children could have grown up in a two-parent home, but the healing came as I saw God moving in my children's lives to provide for them what was lacking. The kids developed an especially close relationship with their grandparents that's rooted in the time we lived at their house after the divorce. God also placed them with the most caring teachers who knew our situation and poured extra love into the kids. In so many ways, I saw how God was going beyond giving us "a bandage" to truly helping us heal and rebuild.

Where is God amidst your heartbreak story? What blessings have you and your children experienced that show how God is faithfully showing up to heal your hearts and help you rebuild?

My journey may be different from yours, but I assure you that God sees you, and He knows your pain. He will make you feel whole once again. It may take time, but you and your children will reach a point where you move beyond the heartbreak.

Jesus, pour out your grace on the kids and me to help us heal and rebuild. Place people in our lives to lift us up and allow me to humbly accept assistance and support from those people.

EPHESIANS 1:18 · MICAH 7:7

2 always loved

"'Though the mountains fall away and the hills be shaken, my love shall never fall away from you nor my covenant of peace be shaken,' says the LORD, who has mercy on you."

— ISAIAH 54:10

It's hard to feel loved in the middle of the mess. When I am surrounded by broken relationships and entrenched in the daily grind of raising children alone while second-guessing the series of events that led to this situation, I sometimes question if I am even lovable at all. Have you ever found yourself so deep in the mess that it seems like God's love for you is different, somehow less, than the love He has for the people whose lives seem to flow smoothly and without problems?

The truth is that God's love for you is beyond anything you can imagine, unconditional and everlasting. He established a covenant with us instead of a contract, so we would grasp the permanence of His deep and abiding love. A contract is merely an exchange of goods or services, and it can be broken if one or both parties do not hold up their end of the deal. A covenant, on the other hand, is the exchange of persons that creates a sacred family, and that family is indissoluble.

There's nothing you can do (or have done) to lose God's love. No matter what, you are His child, and He is your Loving Father.

Experiencing difficulties, even the staggering challenge of parenting alone, does not mean you're unloved. God did not promise you an easy life, but in His mercy, He did promise to love you through these hardships. God longs to step into the mess with you, just as He stepped into the mess of our world and redeemed it on the Cross. Where does life feel messy right now, and how could you invite God to step into that mess with you?

Jesus, please remind me of the breadth, depth, and permanence of Your love for me, all the time... no matter what, and fill me with Your peace.

EZEKIEL 34:25-30 · ZEPHANIAH 3:17

3 never forgotten

"But Zion said, 'The LORD has forsaken me; my Lord has forgotten me.' Can a mother forget her infant, be without tenderness for the child of her womb? Even should she forget, I will never forget you."

— ISAIAH 49:14-15

Isn't it delightful when God chooses to swiftly answer your prayers with a distinct clarity that reassures you that He's listening? When this rarity occurs, you feel particularly seen and heard by your Loving Father, but when you've prayed the same prayer for days, weeks, months, or years without seeing any movement, you might find yourself genuinely feeling like God has forgotten you altogether.

My friend, God has not forgotten you, not even for a minute. In Scripture, God promises over and over that He will not forget you. He knew you and I would have moments of doubt, so He peppered these reminders throughout the Bible. God could never and will never forget you.

Once you embrace this truth, other possibilities for His silent response to your prayer begin to emerge.

- Is God's lack of movement an answer itself, even if you don't like it?
- Is His seeming inactivity a signal that you're focused on the wrong things?
- Is it possible He's simply telling you, "Not yet"?

I know how much I love my own children, and my life is often consumed with careful consideration of how to best meet their needs. I'm sure the same is true for you. But God's love is even more perfect. He is always deeply aware of your prayers and needs, and He's always working to bring about His Will in your life.

Through the silence, God is whispering to you, "Trust Me. I have good plans for you."

In what area(s) of your life do you feel forgotten by God? How is God inviting you to trust Him during this season of waiting?

Jesus, I have waited so long and feel forgotten. Please sustain me in this season of waiting and help me to seek Your will rather than holding tightly to my own desired outcome that may be different than Your perfect plan for me.

ISAIAH 44:21 · PSALM 136:23

---

4 never alone

"I command you: be strong and steadfast! Do not fear nor be dismayed, for the LORD, your God, is with you wherever you go."

— JOSHUA 1:9

As a single parent, you face fears and heartaches that other parents never experience. In particular, the loss of time with your kids due to the visitation schedule.

No matter how many times it happens, watching my kids wave from the other parent's car as they disappear down the road for a week at the other house will always break my heart. When I walk back inside after saying goodbye, I am hit with a deafening silence, a gnawing feeling that something is missing, and the overwhelming sense that I am utterly alone.

Parents are not meant to be separated from their children for extended periods of time. The younger your kids are, the more painful this separation can feel. If you feel like the days without your kids are hollow and muted, no matter what you do to try to fill the void, you are not alone.

Other parents say things to me like, "Aren't you lucky for time alone and a day free from the chores of parenthood?" without realizing how difficult it is for me to enjoy that freedom when I look into the darkness of my children's rooms and feel like a piece of my heart is missing.

Do the days without your kids feel dark? Jesus is there with you in that darkness and has compassion for your pain. He understands the weight of this cross, and He will not abandon you to carry it alone. Jesus is holding you and your kids close during any separation, and He will provide you with the strength to endure until your home is once again filled with your kids' laughter and light.

How could you seek Jesus for support and strength as you cope with missing your kids while they are gone? I don't know what this might look like for you, but I do know that the separation is more bearable when you allow Jesus into the experience with you.

Jesus, please be with me in the void left when my children are gone. Give me the strength to endure this unbearable and unwelcome separation from my children. Help me to use this time to catch up on work, chores, time with You, time with friends, or even rest, so I can be replenished and prepared for when my kids return.

PSALM 46:7 · PSALM 25:16-17

---

5 grieving

"Though my flesh and my heart fail, God is the rock of my heart, my portion forever."

— PSALM 73:26

Whether you're new to the single parent life or you've been in the game for a decade, it's natural to experience grief over the loss of the life you thought you'd have. This is a significant loss, and it triggers grief that needs to be felt and processed.

When I became a single parent, I was devastated to the point of feeling numb. Rather than face the overwhelming emotions under the surface, I poured myself into caring for the kids and into work. People complimented me on how well I was holding it together, but deep down, I was afraid that if I allowed myself to dive into the pain and sorrow, I might never come back up.

A friend saw the pain in my eyes and convinced me that it was time to let myself "feel the feelings." The next time I was alone, I finally allowed the feelings to bubble up.

There were tears. There was singing of praise and worship songs through the tears. There was shouting and pacing the floor as I said the things I needed to say, even though no one but God could hear me. There was angry cardio at the gym. There was curling up in a ball under the covers and more tears. After exhausting my tears and my anger, I took a deep breath, the kind you have when you are emotionally and physically spent. I could feel God holding me extra close as I lay at His feet, completely broken. I didn't let it all go that day, but it was a start.

There are stages of grief, and this process will look different depending on which stage of grief you're in. Is it time to let yourself grieve the life that could have been? What would help you work through and release the feelings? How can you invite God into the process?

Jesus, I feel shattered over the loss of the life I thought I'd have, and the grief keeps coming in waves. Please hold me close as I mourn the life that I lost, and please help me see that, even though my life will be different than I imagined, I will find my way out of this grief if I cling to You.

JOHN 16:22 · MATTHEW 5:4

6 be not afraid

"For I am the LORD, your God, who grasp your right hand;
It is I who say to you, 'Do not fear, I will help you.'"

— ISAIAH 41:13

This may be my favorite verse of the entire Old Testament. A dear friend recommended it to me on a day when it felt like my world was falling apart, and it has become my "go to" verse when crisis hits. You can cling to these words all the time, but especially when fear creeps in because you feel lost, overwhelmed, or hopeless. There's so much to unpack in this one verse.

First, God reminds you that He is grasping your hand.
To grasp means to "seize and hold firmly." This is not a loose grip. God is purposefully grabbing your hand and holding you close. It's okay if you're so worn down that you feel like you can't hold on because the King of the Universe is grasping onto you.

Second, God commands you NOT to fear.
He doesn't say, "Try not to worry." God says, "Do not fear…" He is commanding you to have faith and trust instead of giving into the temptation to dwell in fear. One way to obey God's call to be free from fear is to simply utter, "Jesus, I trust in you." By speaking or meditating on these words, you rein in the fearful thoughts and better position yourself to recognize the possible solutions God is presenting to you.

Third, God promises to help you.
He doesn't say that He might help you. He says He *will* help you. It's always easier to endure something difficult when we know for certain that help is on the way. God's promise to help isn't a promise that bad things will never happen, but it is a promise that, even if the worst-case scenario comes to pass, He will help you find your way through it. This promise keeps hope alive.

What fear is keeping you up at night or distracting you during the day? Which truth from this verse speaks to your heart today and could help you move out of fear and into hope?

Jesus, please plant this scripture in my heart so that I recognize my fears as they surface and immediately lay those anxious thoughts at Your feet. Replace my fears with the comfort of Your promises to hold me and help me.

PSALM 63:9 · 2 CORINTHIANS 10:4-5

7 surrender and soar

"They that hope in the LORD will renew their strength, they will soar on eagles' wings; They will run and not grow weary, walk and not grow faint."

— ISAIAH 40:31

There are days when it's all just too much. I find myself weary to the bone and struggling to take the next step. I bet you've been there too and might even be at that point today. It's a level of exhaustion that makes you feel like washing one more dish or even reading one more story is just too much.

Being the sole breadwinner and the sole caretaker is like running a sprint and a marathon at the same time. You sprint through each day attempting to squeeze in every To-Do item for the home, kids, and work, but unlike most sprints that end quickly, you also have to sustain this pace over a prolonged duration of time. It's understandable that you sometimes start to doubt that you have what it takes to finish the race.

In these moments, you may feel tempted to hold tightly to your To-Do list and power through it alone, but God is inviting you to pass it to Him. There is peace that comes from surrendering to the exhaustion and handing the list to God. Through your obedience and trust, you leave space for God to move.

Have you ever heard the saying, "Let go, and let God"? There's a magical shift that happens when you pause to gather yourself and reconnect with God before continuing your activities. Even five minutes of quiet and stillness can help you recharge, and you can follow that with a prayer asking God to help you know where to push through today and what to leave for another day. With His help, you'll be able to better discern where to spend your limited time and energy, and you'll end up accomplishing more than you could have alone.

What do you need to hand over to God today so He can help you soar?

Jesus, please remind me to cease the endless striving and allow You to carry me. Give me strength and replenish my weary body, mind, heart, and soul, so I can continue the race and finish strong.

DEUTERONOMY 31:6 · EXODUS 15:2

8 the hero

"But thanks be to God who gives us the victory through our Lord Jesus Christ."

— 1 CORINTHIANS 15:57

Today, I'd like to pause for a moment and celebrate you. Yes—YOU!

To your kids and to so many others, you are a hero. It doesn't matter how exhausted you are. Every day, by God's grace, you show up for your kids in so many ways.

- You sacrifice your time and energy to compassionately care for them.
- You work hard to provide for them, even if it means working in a job with steady income that may not be your dream job.
- You manage the finances and balance meeting the needs of today with preparing to meet the needs of tomorrow.
- You make sure they have what they need to grow and thrive, including food, good hygiene, exercise, healthy habits, and sleep.
- You pay attention to what makes your children unique, shine a light on their talents, and provide opportunities for them to develop those talents.
- You wipe their noses, and you wipe away their tears.
- You teach them about God's love and mercy.
- You manage all of the household chores, including scrubbing dishes, cleaning the house, caring for the pets, washing laundry, and taking out the trash.
- You provide or coordinate all the rides to school and activities.
- You take an interest in your kids' lives and support them in their academics and extracurriculars.
- You laugh and play and teach your kids to dream.
- You show your kids how much they are loved. And you tell them, too.

You are carrying a load that is meant for two people. Under the weight of such a heavy responsibility, others might have crumbled, but you have persevered.

One day at a time, (and sometimes even one hour at a time), you choose to keep fighting for, protecting, and uplifting your kids.

You are a HERO.

When was the last time you acknowledged the tremendous load that you carry and how gracefully you carry it (most of the time)? When was the last time you celebrated and thanked God for these victories, big or small?

Jesus, thank You for giving me this moment to reflect on the heroic nature of my efforts to raise my children without a spouse. I know every victory comes from You, and I ask that You continue to help me persevere and show up in every way for my kids.

ROMANS 8:37 · PSALM 60:14

---

9 dare to dream

"Not only that, but we even boast of our afflictions, knowing that affliction produces endurance, and endurance, proven character, and proven character, hope, and hope does not disappoint, because the love of God has been poured out into our hearts through the Holy Spirit that has been given to us."

— ROMANS 5:3-5

Have you ever paused to consider how God is using your experience as a single parent to reveal a larger purpose for your life?

It's easy to become so wrapped up in pushing through the busy days that you forget—one day there will be more. One day, your children will not need you as much as they do now. Slowly but surely, your time will again become your own.

Then what?

Currently, you might feel like that point is too far off to even contemplate what's next. I mean, right now, you might just settle for going to the bathroom or taking a shower without interruption. But give yourself permission, just for a moment, to honestly consider what might be next for you when this part of your life becomes less demanding.

I'd be willing to bet that you will not be the same person at that future time that you once were when you became a single parent. I know I'm not. Even now, I can see how this journey is changing me. I'm happy to report that, in many ways, I believe it's for the better, and I imagine the same is true for you too.

Parenting, particularly parenting solo, produces endurance and shapes your character. If you allow Him to, God will use this experience to prepare and reveal a larger purpose for your life beyond surviving and raising good children.

Pope John XXIII once said, "Consult not your fears but your hopes and your dreams. Think not about your frustrations, but about your unfulfilled potential. Concern yourself not with what you tried and failed in, but with what it is still possible for you to do."

Don't be afraid to hope and dream. God still has big plans for you.

How has being a single parent changed you for the better? What seeds has God started planting in your heart and mind that hint at His purpose for your life once the kids require less of your time?

Jesus, I know You're changing me for the better in many ways through my journey as a single parent. Please fill me with new hopes and dreams for the future that align with Your renewed purpose for my life and help me follow where You lead.

1 PETER 6:7 · JAMES 1:2-4

---

10 chosen

"'But now,' thus says the LORD, 'who created you, Jacob, and formed you, Israel: Do not fear, for I have redeemed you; I have called you by name: you are mine.'"

— ISAIAH 43:1

Even if you know that becoming a single parent was your best option in a difficult situation, you probably still have days where you feel consumed by guilt, fear, shame, or rejection that leave you feeling unworthy, unwanted, and unsure of where you fit in. I know I do, and on these days, I ache for a sense of belonging.

Maybe everyone in your friend group is married, and they tend to socialize with other couples. They don't mean to exclude you, but that doesn't change the fact that you feel rejected when you find out they didn't invite you. You long to belong.

Maybe at school events, you feel embarrassed as you sit alone with no one to talk to while the other parents sit with their spouses and enjoy the events together. Logically, you know that no one thinks less of you because you're there alone, but that doesn't erase the feeling that you don't fit in. You long to belong.

Maybe you're struggling to find your place at church. From the homilies to the faith formation to the various ministries to the activities like the church picnic, everything is geared toward married couples and families. Even the "singles" groups are geared toward younger singles who have not yet married or had kids. There is likely nothing to specifically support or welcome single parents. You long to belong.

In these moments, you can turn to one of the most loving and comforting statements made by God in all of scripture: "Do not fear, for I have redeemed you; I have called you by name; you are mine."

There are no conditions on His love. He accepts and adores you just as you are.

You are known, loved, and redeemed. You belong, especially at church, and you are His.

How is God calling you to live in the freedom and joy of knowing you belong to Him? How might this truth enable you to redefine your sense of belonging in other areas of your life?

Jesus, please remind me that I am chosen by You and that, regardless of my situation, I belong to You and with You. Fill me with unwavering faith that You have called me by name and that I am Yours, now and always.

PSALM 100:3 · JOHN 10:27-28

11 seeking God

"When you call me, and come and pray to me,
I will listen to you. When you look for me, you will find me.
Yes, when you seek me with all your heart..."

— JEREMIAH 29:12-13

Some days, God seems so close. You feel the joy and peace that comes from knowing He is near. Other days, God feels far away, and you struggle to muster up any joy or peace as you force yourself to push through the exhaustion and pressure to do all of this alone.

It can feel like you're just going through the motions only to do it all again the next day. God seems distant, and life feels like a grind.

You've probably heard the saying, "Seek, and you will find." But there's a caveat. God calls us to seek Him with all our hearts, and *then* we will surely find Him.

When I read (and reread) that passage from Jeremiah, I came to understand that when God seems far away, it's usually because I have been so busy surviving that I've forgotten to seek Him.

What does it really mean to seek God with all your heart? It could certainly mean taking drastic action to focus your every thought and word on Him, but God also leaves room for more subtle efforts that you could make to pursue Him as you go about your daily routine.

You might offer a mundane chore, such as unloading the dishwasher or folding laundry, as a prayer. You might catch yourself when you start to complain and find something to be grateful for instead, particularly for things that you usually take for granted. You might reorient your prayers to focus on understanding God's will instead of explaining what you want. You might offer Him a part of your life that you've previously held back because you feared what He might ask of you.

Seeking after God with all your heart, mind, and soul enables you to become more aware of the big and small ways He is showing up amidst your busyness. Suddenly, God doesn't seem so far away.

At any given moment, God is near and inviting you to call on Him. If God feels distant today, it's time to ask yourself, "Am I seeking God *with all my heart*?" If not, what would it look like to seek God with your whole heart today?

Jesus, I know you are near, but I don't feel close to you today. Please hear my call and show me how I can seek you with my whole heart.

MATTHEW 22:37 · ISAIAH 55:6

12 **thanks in advance**

"In all circumstances give thanks, for this is the will of God for you in Christ Jesus."

— 1 THESSALONIANS 5:18

In ALL circumstances give thanks? Seems borderline impossible, doesn't it?

When the other parent does something to upset you and disrupt the kids' routine, such as introducing the kids to a new dating partner or announcing that he or she will be moving to another state and changing the visitation, your first thought probably isn't to be thankful or rejoice. In fact, gratitude may be the last thing on your mind.

My kids and I have walked through this experience more than once. The first time this happened, I shook my fist at God and asked, "Why would you allow this to happen to us?! We've been through so much already. You could have spared us this pain, but You didn't. Why?!"

Then, I looked at the picture of Michelangelo's *Pieta* on my dresser and remembered that even Jesus' mother, Mary, endured heart-wrenching pain and devastating loss. Let that sink in. If Mother Mary was allowed to suffer so profoundly despite God's deep love for her, you can be sure that God's love for you and your kids prevails despite the challenges you're facing.

If you're in this season with your kids, you may be tempted to blame God for not preventing your seemingly unbearable situation. It's understandable that you would feel this way. God understands when we get upset and question Him, but what if God is actually using this circumstance to invite you to trust Him more completely than you've ever trusted Him before?

Offering gratitude despite what is happening around you is a powerful act of trust. This is not a flippant suggestion to look on the bright side when your world is falling apart. If you are grateful, even in difficult circumstances, it can transform the way you experience all of life.

The next time you feel tempted to grow angry at God for your circumstances, try making a gratitude list. Pause and take a moment to write down two or three things you are grateful for, big or small. You might even thank God ahead of time for blessings He may bestow on you and your kids during this difficult transition.

Jesus, I don't understand why this is happening, and it's hard to remember that this pain will eventually pass. Lift my heart and soul above these circumstances so I can let go of my anger and focus on thanking You ahead of time for the various ways you will sustain us through this season.

EPHESIANS 6:18 · PSALM 86:2-4

13 known and loved

"Blessed be the LORD, marvelously he showed to me his mercy in a fortified city. Though I had said in my alarm, 'I am cut off from your eyes.' Yet you heard my voice, my cry for mercy, when I pleaded with you for help."

— PSALM 31:22-23

Sick kid. Work deadline. Broken washing machine. All at the same time and all at the worst possible time.

When my day unravels this way, or worse, when I seem to be in a cycle of bad luck for weeks or months, I find myself crying out to God and saying, "I'm working so hard to juggle all of this. It's bad enough I have to do it all alone. Could I *please* just catch a break?"

I imagine you've been there too. It's that moment when it all just feels like too much. You feel like you can't take on one more problem, but then, *boom*, one more problem lands in your lap.

It's enough to make you ask God, "Do you even see me?"

The answer to whether or not He sees you is a resounding, "YES!" Even in the moments when you feel like you just can't catch a break, God sees you and hears you. When you find yourself sinking into despair, you can begin to pull yourself out by looking for God's providence in the chaos.

How is He caring for you through the problem, even if He doesn't remove the problem? When I ask myself this question, it puts a whole new spin on how I view what is happening around me.

Without the sick kid, I may not have been home to catch the issue with the washer before it caused a flood, and I may not have discovered my co-worker's kindness and willingness to help me meet the deadline. God's response to our pleas often takes the form of fortifying us against problems that we didn't even know were looming ahead.

You and I view life through the lens of past feelings and experiences that shapes our perspective on our current situation. It's easy to let past hurt and disappointment taint your view, but when you sense this happening, try looking at your situation again through the lens of certainty that God sees you and loves you. This perspective changes everything.

When you operate from this assumption, you're more attuned to the blessings amidst the burdens. Instead of feeling hidden from God, you can feel seen, known, and loved, even during tough times.

How is God using your disappointments and frustrations to speak to you? How is He using them to serve a greater purpose for your benefit?

Jesus, so many things have gone wrong lately that I've found myself wondering if you even see or hear me. Please shift my gaze from the problems around me to the vast goodness You may be working for me through these challenges.

LUKE 12:6-7 · PSALM 27:7

14 **time to play**

"May the God of hope fill you with all joy and peace in believing, so that you may abound in hope by the power of the Holy Spirit."

— ROMANS 15:13

When's the last time your home was filled with JOY—pure, unadulterated joy and laughter?

If your response is, "I don't know," you're not alone. Some weeks, it feels like I'm constantly nagging, the kids are constantly whining, and we're just grinding through and trying to survive. I don't know about you, but that is not the childhood I want for my kids.

When I notice we're caught in this rut, I know it's time to lighten things up. Perhaps it's time for you to do the same. It's clear from Scripture that God's desire is for you and your children to be filled with joy.

One of my favorite television series ever is called *The Chosen*. In Season 1, there is a scene in which Jesus is genuinely playful and silly with two children. It moved me to tears as I contemplated the humanity of Jesus. It was a beautiful scene that prompted me to think about the importance of joy and laughter in dealing with my own kids.

You know what will work best to spark joy and play in your family, but if you need suggestions on how to lighten things up with your kids, you might try one of these:

- Crank up a favorite song (the sillier and more unexpected the better) and start a kitchen dance party
- Catch the kids off guard by spraying someone with the kitchen sprayer (and be a good sport when they get you back)
- Respond to a stressful situation with your child with humor instead of anger or frustration
- Randomly tell your child something you love about him or her
- Turn off the TV and have a family game night

Bringing the silly back doesn't mean letting your kids get away with bad behavior, but it does break the tension and bring the joy back to your home. It also lays the foundation for a productive conversation with your kids later about behavior expectations and how you can all work to keep the house filled with joy.

Jesus had many important things to do during His ministry, but He paused that important work to play with the children and bring them joy. He's inviting you to do the same. What adjustment could you make this week to bring more joy to your home?

Jesus, inspire me to inject more joy and happiness into the interactions I have with my kids. Give me and the kids a genuine joy that can only come from knowing You and fill our home with laughter.

PSALM 118:23-24 · PSALM 63:5-6

15 quiet time

"But when you pray, go to your inner room, close the door, and pray to your Father in secret. And your Father who sees in secret will repay you."

— MATTHEW 6:6

It can feel like a luxury to find time alone to pray when you have kids, especially when you're the only parent in the house. The best time for me to pray is before the kids wake up, and I've found that to be the case with many parents. If you're like me, it's tempting to hit "snooze" on the alarm and postpone praying until sometime later in the day, but that quiet time never seems to materialize once the kids are up and the day starts rolling.

Carving out even ten minutes with Jesus before the kids wake up makes a world of difference in my day. I sip my coffee, read my Bible, journal about my favorite verses, and contemplate how God is speaking to me through His Word. I talk with Jesus about anything that comes to mind and soak up the peace that comes from lingering in His presence.

Time with Him in the stillness of the morning grounds me and sets my focus for the day on what is above instead of the endless list of activities in front of me. Despite rising earlier, I have more energy as I step into my day aware of Jesus' presence with me.

On the days when I skip my "quiet time" with Jesus, I'm more scattered and anxious, and it is much easier for Satan to draw me into negative thoughts, fear, and self-condemnation. It's as though the extra sleep costs me my peace for the rest of the day.

Scripture tells us that Jesus often went to the mountains by Himself to pray. If the Son needed quiet time alone with the Father to pray, surely we benefit as much as Jesus did, if not more, from making quiet time alone with God a priority in our lives too.

Do you make time alone with God a priority in your daily routine? If not, what adjustment could you make to your routine to allow for this nourishing, uplifting, soul-fueling time with God in your day? If you already do this, what do you cherish about this routine, and how could you bump it up a notch to engage even more with God during this time?

Jesus, I'm humbled and in awe that the King of the Universe chooses to spend time alone with me. Please give me the grace to make quiet time with you a priority in my life and fill me with clarity and peace during our time together.

MATTHEW 14:23 · LUKE 6:12

16 **reluctant gratitude**

"Though I am afflicted and poor, my Lord keeps me in mind. You are my help and deliverer; my God, do not delay!"

— PSALM 40:18

A single parent's prayer often sounds more like, "Thank You, God, that it wasn't worse," than, "Thank You, God, for that perfect outcome."

When the kids and I were stuck on a deserted road with a flat tire or when I hear stories about the kids' time at the other house where things are handled differently than they are at home, sometimes, being thankful it wasn't worse is the best I can do. In His mercy, God recognizes this as a genuine prayer of gratitude even if I occasionally allow a bitter tone to creep in.

The Bible stories about how Jesus helped and healed people on the spot are beautiful. They fill us with anticipation and faith that Jesus will do the same for us. But on the days when all I can find to be grateful for is that it wasn't worse, the Psalms and other Old Testament stories filled with lament and cries to God for restoration and healing resonate in my soul.

When you have a day like this, you can call on the Holy Spirit for help with your prayers. In Romans 8:26, God tells us that the Holy Spirit will intercede for us when we can't quite find the words, including the days when our tone leans more toward bitterness and angst than genuine joy and gratitude.

"In the same way, the Spirit too comes to the aid of our weakness; for we do not know how to pray as we ought, but the Spirit itself intercedes with inexpressible groanings."

What trial or affliction has you thanking God that it's not worse and calling out to God in lament with pleas for swift deliverance? Why not pause now to ask the Holy Spirit to intercede for you as you struggle to express genuine gratitude?

Jesus, in the midst of unanticipated problems, please remind me to call on the Holy Spirit for intercession when I struggle to find words of gratitude. Help me to express genuine gratitude for Your assistance, even if all I can muster is a, "Thank You, God, that it wasn't worse."

DEUTERONOMY 28:2 · JAMES 1:7

17 grasping for control

"In danger I called on the LORD;
the LORD answered me and set me free."

— PSALM 118:5

Nothing makes me feel more helpless than when it's the other parent's time and I'm not in control of what's happening with my own children. Whether your child's other parent is involved or not, there will inevitably come a time when you don't agree with the influences that other people bring into your kids' lives, and you may feel helpless to stop it, especially as they get older.

To be clear, *I am not referring to emotional or physical abuse. If you're in an abusive situation of any kind, please know that you can and should seek help to stop the abuse.* I'm referring to situations that may be allowed by law but fall well outside of what you believe is right, such as the other parent introducing the kids to ever-changing dating partners or someone leading your kids away from the Church. You feel this is detrimental to your kids, but you are not in a position to change what's happening.

However much you hope and pray, the situation you'd give anything to stop may still come to pass. In losing all control, we are left with no other option but to hand the situation over to God, and when we make that choice, He often shows up mightily to remind us that we can trust Him, always.

On a particularly rough weekend apart from the kids, I felt helpless because I knew they were facing a distressing situation. It was an experience that I never would have chosen for them, and I could do nothing to stop it because it wasn't "my" weekend. My only recourse in that moment was prayer. I begged God to protect and comfort the kids, and I asked Him to ease the desperate ache inside of me to be with them.

In search of comfort, I decided to venture out for coffee and quiet time to journal. I chose a restaurant in another city, thinking that a change of scenery would help. As I sat at my table blinking back the tears and scribbling my thoughts down on paper, I heard a little voice whisper, "Mom!"

I looked up, and there across the table I saw my beautiful babies staring back at me. I couldn't believe my eyes! For a moment, we just smiled at each other with surprise and delight, and then, I wrapped my arms around them for a hug that I will never forget.

I was in awe of what God had done for us. Somehow, in an area with thousands of restaurants, we had ended up at the same place. Yet, I knew this was no coincidence. It was one of the most immediate and powerful answers to prayer that I've ever experienced. That day, God showed up mightily to remind me that He will protect my children even when I can't and that I can always rely on Him for rescue, even when all hope seems lost. The same is true for you.

When you feel beaten down by the loss of control over your children's lives, are you able to surrender the situation to your loving Father in faith and trust, or do you continue to grasp for control? How is God inviting you to believe that He will show up for you and your children again and again in your darkest hours?

Jesus, it is heart-wrenching to feel like I can't protect my children from something that I believe is not the best thing for them. Please wrap Your arms around my children and protect them at all times, especially when I can't.

PSALM 40:14 · 2 CORINTHIANS 1:8-10

18 **your story**

"Before I formed you in the womb I knew you, before you were born I dedicated you, a prophet to the nations I appointed you."

— JEREMIAH 1:5

When I read this verse, my mind always jumps to my two beautiful children. I know they were gifts from God, and I'm certain God has a special calling on each of their lives that was established before they were even born. One of my most heartfelt prayers for my kids is that they follow God's will for their lives and fulfill the purpose that He established for them. I imagine you feel the same way about your child(ren).

Now, read the verse again and contemplate how this applies to YOU too. God not only knew you before He formed you in the womb, but He's also had a plan for you even before the foundation of the world. God has always known your story, and His plan for you factors in all of the twists and turns that your life on Earth would take, even your journey as a single parent.

Reflecting on that truth brought me an incredible amount of peace. After my divorce, it felt like I had lost any chance of happiness and peace.

The recurring thought, "I failed at marriage," soon became, "I am a failure," and that soon became, "I failed at my one shot to live God's will for my life." I wish I had recognized sooner that those words did not come from God. God didn't architect my divorce, but He did know it would happen and how to bring good from it.

Your story did not end because you became a single parent. What may have felt like a wrong turn was actually part of your journey all along, and your beautiful children are proof of that. You are where you were meant to be at this time in your life. Worrying about how you're not where you thought you would be doesn't solve anything. Focus your energy on discovering God's calling on your life now that you are here.

How is God calling you to new dreams and new ways of serving others through your experience as a single parent?

Jesus, open my heart and mind to discover the calling You have on my life now, right where I am, and help me to pursue that calling according to Your will.

PHILIPPIANS 1:6 · EPHESIANS 1:4

19 **burden to blessing**

**"Bear one another's burdens,
and so you will fulfill the law of Christ."**

— GALATIANS 6:2

As Christians, we are meant to have an instinct for service, jumping in to help when we see someone in need. Saint Paul tells us that bearing one another's burdens allows us to fulfill the law of Christ.

Why is it, then, that I cringe at the thought of asking for help?

Certainly, there's a bit of pride there because I don't want to admit to others that I need help or expose my mess, but at the heart of the matter, there's a bigger reason why I hesitate to ask for help.

The truth is that I don't want to be a burden to someone else, and maybe, the same is true for you.

When you feel like a burden, you are usually afraid that you're creating extra work, expense, inconvenience, or frustration that may ultimately lead to that person growing tired of helping—or tired of you altogether. But here's the reality—you are a single parent, and there are going to be days when you need help. While you certainly want to be considerate of others and not overstay your welcome, you should be able to ask for help from time to time without the worry that you'll be a burden.

If you feel like your concern about being seen as a burden is holding you back from asking for much-needed assistance, it might be time to consider the root cause of that view. You may be able to figure it out on your own. If not, a good counselor could guide you in exploring and addressing the root cause. You deserve to live in the freedom of believing you are worthy of help and that it's acceptable to ask others for help.

Whether you have a deep resistance to asking for help or just a minor hesitation, a simple mindset shift rooted squarely in Scripture can help you see asking for help in a whole new light. If you carefully read Scripture, you'll see that God's not just telling us to help others. God is telling you that asking someone else to bear your burdens actually allows that person to live their faith and follow God's will for their lives too.

By asking for help now and then, you are actually a blessing, not a burden. Let that sink in for a minute.

Have you been resisting asking for help out of fear of being a burden? If you could view asking for help as a blessing to someone instead of a burden, how would it change your willingness to ask for help or the frequency with which you would do so?

Jesus, I know I need help, but I've been hesitant to ask out of fear of being a burden. Help me to see through Your eyes that I am worthy and that, by asking for help, I can actually be a blessing to someone instead of a burden.

JOHN 13:34 · 1 JOHN 3:16-18

20 loneliness

"Father of the fatherless, defender of widows—God in his holy abode, God gives a home to the forsaken..."

— PSALM 68:6-7

Loneliness is a regular and recurring emotion for many single parents. I am almost never alone, and yet I am always alone. I crave the solace of having a spouse and the intimacy of knowing and being known. My kids and friends are truly enjoyable company, but it's not the same as having a partner to share a life with me now and when the kids are grown and gone.

I've prayed countless prayers asking Jesus to lead me to "the one" He's chosen for me. Yet, after more than a decade, I'm still on my own.

Weekends are the hardest. The frantic weekday routine leaves little time to contemplate my feelings, but on the weekends, reminders that I am alone pop up in almost every activity. You might have experienced this too. Whether you are at the grocery store, the soccer field, a restaurant, or even at church, you're inevitably surrounded by couples and families. And when you're home, particularly on the weekends when the kids are gone, the absence of companionship is palpable as you prepare meals, work in the yard, or sit down to watch a movie on a Saturday night—alone.

Between the seemingly unanswered prayer for a spouse and the lack of companionship, it's easy to fall into the temptation to feel abandoned. On days when I feel particularly lonely, I've found that the best remedy is to spend time at Eucharistic Adoration where Jesus is present in such a tangible way.

In that chapel, I feel like I am home, held, and known. Whether I go for ten minutes or two hours, I walk away feeling comforted and reconnected to the most intimate of all relationships, my relationship with Jesus. I am reminded that I am never truly alone.

In John 1:45-49, Philip invites Nathanael to "come and see" the Messiah. As Nathanael approaches, Jesus immediately speaks about Nathanael as though He already knows him. When Nathanael asks Jesus, "How do you know me?" Jesus explains, "Before Philip called you, I saw you under the fig tree." Without hesitation, Nathanael's immediate response is, "Rabbi, you are the Son of God."

What drove Nathanael to instantly recognize Jesus as the Son of God? Jesus revealed that He was present with Nathanael, even when Nathanael didn't notice Him there. Like Nathanael, you're never alone or forsaken either. With Jesus, you are always home, held, and known, especially on those days when your kids are gone.

When the loneliness creeps in, do you allow Satan to convince you that you've been abandoned or do you run home to Jesus?

Jesus, even when I'm surrounded by a crowd, I feel alone. Fill me with the joy of knowing that I belong to you and that, in You, I am always home, held, and known.

PSALM 146:9 · EXODUS 22:21-22

21 it's all temporary

"For this momentary light affliction is producing for us an eternal weight of glory beyond all comparison, as we look not to what is seen but to what is unseen; for what is seen is transitory, but what is unseen is eternal."

— 2 CORINTHIANS 4:17-18

What's the most difficult age to parent? I imagine we could debate that topic for days. What I do know is that becoming a single parent with two kids under the age of two was one of the most difficult challenges I've ever faced. I was beyond sleep-deprived, stretched thin as I worked to provide for us and care for them, and in a constant state of worry over how I could make a good, stable life for my kids as a single parent. I kept thinking it would get easier when they were a little older.

In some ways, it has, but as you know all too well, whatever the age your kids may be, a single parent carries a particularly heavy burden. Your affliction may take the form of financial strain, the ever-present juggling of responsibilities at home and work, loneliness, stress, exhaustion from handling most of the day-to-day responsibilities of raising your kids alone, or maybe all of the above.

When you hit the point where it all just feels like too much, it can help to remember that God has promised us that "this" is temporary. Whatever "this" is, it is temporary.

It may not necessarily be short-term, but "this" will end eventually. Saint Padre Pio once said, "To the extent that Jesus wants to raise a soul to perfection, He then increases the cross of tribulation." If you allow God to work on you and through you during this difficult time, He can use this affliction to change you for the better.

How has your experience as a single parent changed you? How might God be using the challenges of being a single parent to refine you and bring you closer to Him?

Jesus, give me the perseverance to endure my suffering and the humility to accept this opportunity to be refined and perfected according to Your will. Help me remember that this is temporary.

JAMES 1: 2-4 · 2 CORINTHIANS 1:8-9

---

22 **anxious thoughts**

"I am with you and will protect you wherever you go and bring you back to this land. I will never leave you until I have done what I promised you."

— GENESIS 28:15

The day I filed for divorce, all I could think was, "This is not the life I wanted for my children." How would growing up in a single parent home affect them? Would I be able to do this alone? Would we be okay? Would the three of us ever feel like a "complete" family again?

You may be wrestling with your own version of "This is not the life I wanted for my children," and all the fears about the future that come with that.

The menacing thoughts keep you up at night when you should be sleeping and distract you when you should be working. They steal your joy.

From time to time, we all give into this temptation to imagine all that could go wrong down the road, which is exactly what Satan wants. Satan wants you so consumed with fear about all that could go wrong in the future that you miss out on the beauty, joy, and peace in front of you today, including precious time with your kids.

Be aware of your thoughts. When the fears start piling up, you know you're under attack from the enemy. In that moment, Jesus wants you to lay it all down at His feet.

Take a deep breath in. Exhale slowly. And then redirect your mind to God's truth.

Jesus is with you and has promised that He will never leave you. He has promised to bring you back to a place where you feel steady and complete.

Whatever the future may bring, He will either protect you and your children from it or guard you as you walk through it. Life is too short to dwell on future problems, especially those that may never come to pass.

What fear is Satan tempting you to focus on today? What truth from God do you need to speak over that fear?

Jesus, please banish from my mind all temptation to fear the future. Replace those thoughts with laser focus on the present moment and on all of the ways in which you are protecting and providing for me and my children today.

PSALM 46:2 · PSALM 145:18-19

---

23 **you belong**

"So then you are no longer strangers and sojourners, but you are fellow citizens with the holy ones and members of the household of God, built upon the foundation of the apostles and prophets, with Christ Jesus himself as the capstone."

— EPHESIANS 2:19-20

If you've found a thriving single parent community or support for single parents at your church, you should buy a lottery ticket. Seriously. That's like hitting the jackpot.

Unfortunately, single parent communities and support for single parents are basically non-existent at most parishes. In my experience, the parishes, and even the diocese as a whole, tend to focus on grief support for single parents more than on welcoming single parents and ensuring they know that they are a valued part of the parish community.

I once tried to start a single parent group at my church and was told not to bother because, even if I opened it up to people in the surrounding parishes, there would not be enough single parents to form a group. All I could think was, "That's your Christian response to a lonely soul longing for community?! I know I'm not the only single parent in our diocese of 1.2 million people."

It's enough to make you feel like you don't belong at church. If you've ever felt that way, you're not alone, but please hear me when I tell you that couldn't be further from the truth.

According to Pew Research*, Catholic parents who are divorced, separated, widowed, or never married make up 21 percent of all Catholic parents in the United States. We are equally valuable members and are equally called to participate and raise our children in the faith. You are not alone.

You've likely found that people in the pews respond in a variety of ways to seeing that you are a single parent. Some give you a compassionate smile but stay at a distance. Others look down on you with judgment even though they don't know your story and have no right to judge. Starting right now, don't give those people another thought. They aren't living their faith if they are judging you.

No matter what, Jesus is overjoyed that you are there. He can use your strong faith in the face of difficulties to inspire others. He can use your carefully honed emotional intelligence to recognize those in need of encouragement and lift them up. He can use your experience as a resource to help someone else just beginning their journey as a single parent.

Hold your head high. Be visible and involved. You are loved, and you belong.

How is Jesus calling you to let go of any embarrassment you have about your single parent status and to become more engaged in your church community? How are you uniquely equipped to serve your church community?

*2014 U.S. Religious Landscape Study - Parents of children under 18 among Catholics

Jesus, thank You for reminding me that I'm not the only Catholic single parent out there and that I belong in Your Church. Please help me find my place, my contribution, and my people within the parish community.

ROMANS 1:11-12 · PSALM 27:10

24 blessed and protected

"The LORD will guard you from all evil; he will guard your soul. The LORD will guard your coming and going both now and forever."

— PSALM 121:7-8

One of my favorite memories with the kids is floating together in the ocean on a trip to the beach. No chores. No schedule. Just pure joy and being in the moment together as we gently rocked in the waves.

Of course, I was tempted to worry while we were in the water. There was a little nagging voice in my head saying, "What about riptides and sharks?" But as we bobbed in the water that day, I knew God wanted me to trust in His protection and simply savor this special time with my kids.

That's what parenting is really all about, trusting God to keep your children safe as you help them grow into the people God is calling them to be. You and I are called to teach our kids how to step out into the world and try new things with confidence in God's protection. Gradually, we have to let them go. The only way to find peace with that is to turn your children over to God's care and protection.

The instinct to hold on and protect is heightened for us as single parents for many reasons. Any parent wants to protect their kids, but when you know the consequences of the outcome rest squarely on your shoulders, the stakes are higher. If something goes wrong, not only is your child impacted, but your already limited time and resources might be impacted too. Worse yet, a problem might spark a painful, or even blame-filled, discussion with the other parent about your choices and ability to parent.

Knowing how high the stakes are can make it hard to find the right balance between holding on and letting go. When you feel the weight of this responsibility, it's time to pray and trust God more than ever.

Can you imagine how Mary felt as she raised Jesus and encouraged His mission, all the while knowing the suffering ahead for both of them? Yet, she trusted God's plan and protection. What a beautiful example of what it means to entrust your children to God's care.

I remind myself of this on a daily basis by saying the following prayer with my kids each morning when we get in the car: "God, please bless us and protect us in all that we do today. Please let your angels wrap their wings around us and keep us safe, especially on the road, at work, at school, and at our activities. In the name of the Father, and of the Son, and of the Holy Spirit. Amen."

I invite you to try that prayer with your kids too. Calling on God's promise of protection for you and your children will allow you and your kids to more confidently take healthy risks and try new things.

In what area is God calling you to entrust your children more fully to His protection?

Jesus, please help me release my children into your care as they independently step out into the world. Show me where to hold on and where to let go so that my children can gain the experience that will mold them into the people you're calling them to be.

PSALM 91:11-12 · PSALM 139:9-10

25 **making plans**

"Many are the plans of the human heart, but it is the decision of the LORD that endures."

— PROVERBS 19:21

I don't know about you, but my response to God often sounds more like, "Here I am, Lord, and here's how I'd like this to go," than simply, "Here I am. I am ready to do Your will." It's one thing to say that we are open to God's plan for our lives. It's quite another to put those words into action!

I've caused a great deal of strife in my own life by trying to force my own plans instead of asking God what the plan should be, actively listening for His direction, and responding accordingly. At times, I haven't even invited God into my planning process. And worse yet, there have been times when I've convinced myself that because I was able to make something happen, it must have been God's will, even though there were so many indicators to the contrary.

A great example of this was my choice to marry someone who was not Catholic. Despite the clear indicators that having different faiths would be a strain on the relationship, I moved forward with the engagement and wedding because I was ready to be married and have kids. I was convinced God would help us sort it out later despite my family and friends telling me they weren't sure how this marriage could work.

If I had paused long enough to ask God what His plan was for me and if I had gone into the conversation willing to follow His plan even if it didn't align with mine, I'm quite certain I never would have gotten married. My faith is a huge part of my life, and the right partner for me would have to share my faith in order to support me in pursuing God's calling for my life. Unfortunately, I never invited God into that conversation. Thankfully, He still brought something beautiful from my disobedience, my children, but on a personal level, I've still paid a price for going off course.

Scripture is clear that God should be in charge of the plans and that those who follow the way of the Lord will have life and prosper. Embracing this hard-earned wisdom has changed how I live and make decisions, and if you're not already approaching your decision-making in this way, this could be a game-changer for you too.

As a single parent, you can probably look back at some point in your past when you pursued your own plans instead of God's plan. In hindsight, it's probably easy to see how things might have turned out differently if you had invited God into your planning process. It's a radical shift to hand the planning back to its rightful owner and to follow where He leads. It sounds so simple, but it takes intention to live this way.

Is there an area of your life in which you're trying to hold onto control of the plans or force a particular outcome regardless of what God may want for you? If so, why? And what would it look like to hand that situation back to God and follow where He leads?

Jesus, open my heart and mind to seeking and pursing God's plan for my life instead of the plan I might like to choose for myself, particularly if my plans are in conflict with what God wants for me. Help me to instead say, "Here I am Lord. I am ready to do your will."

DEUTERONOMY 5:32-33 · ISAIAH 48:17-18

26 **speak life**

"Death and life are in the power of the tongue; those who choose one shall eat its fruit."

— PROVERBS 18:21

The life of a single parent is filled with a lot of "too much" and "not enough" all at the same time. Too much to do and not enough time. Too much running and not enough rest. And sometimes more overwhelming scenarios like, too many mouths to feed and not enough food.

I don't know about you, but falling into the habit of complaining about all of this "too much" and "not enough" is a very slippery slope for me. Have you found yourself falling into this same trap?

Scripture tells us that our words have real power, and the words we choose either speak life or death over our situation. King Solomon mentions the power of the tongue and of our words more than fifty times in the Book of Proverbs alone. Matthew's Gospel tells us, "For from the fullness of the heart the mouth speaks" (Matthew 12:34). Complaining traps us and prevents us from experiencing the abundant life Jesus offers to us.

Although you and I have probably heard these Scriptures, how often do we think about the power of our words as they spill out of our mouths—and about what those words reveal about our hearts? I'm the first to admit that I do not reflect on the power of my words or intentionally choose my words as often as I should.

Science has also proven that complaining has a negative impact on our well-being. Complaining rewires your brain for negativity, and it damages your health by releasing higher cortisol, which increases your risk of developing heart disease, high cholesterol, diabetes, obesity, and strokes.

For the sake of your physical and spiritual health, it's time to focus on "speaking life" over your life and your children's lives. Thankfully, Saint Paul tells us in Philippians 4:18 exactly where to start:

> *"Finally, brothers, whatever is true, whatever is honorable, whatever is just, whatever is pure, whatever is lovely, whatever is gracious, if there is any excellence and if there is anything worthy of praise, think about these things."*

I've found that the easiest way to speak life is to simply replace the "not enough" and the "too much" with "thank you." Gratitude doesn't eliminate what is hard, but it silences the temptation to complain and immediately reconnects us with the fruit of the Spirit: love, joy, peace, patience, kindness, generosity, faithfulness, gentleness, self-control.

In what area are you and/or your kids trapped in a habit of negative thinking or complaining? How is God inviting you to be a role model and leader for your family by speaking life over that part of your lives?

Jesus, help me to consciously catch negative thoughts and words before they spill out and inspire me to instead speak life over all areas of my life and my children's lives.

MATTHEW 12:34-35 · 1 PETER 3:10-11

27 grace under pressure

"I have told you this so that you might have peace in me. In the world you will have trouble, but take courage, I have conquered the world."

— JOHN 16:33

I will never forget the first time the kids' dad brought his new girlfriend to a family gathering. It was Halloween, and the only way I could go trick-or-treating with my kids was to invite their dad, who brought his girlfriend. For the kids' sake, I smiled through the tears when I was asked to take a picture of my own children, my ex-husband, and his girlfriend, as though they were the family, and I was an outsider.

Navigating the strained family dynamics at your children's special events can be painful for everyone involved, and it becomes even more complicated when one or both parents have a new significant other.

Have you crossed this bridge yet? If you have, you know it's a strange and humiliating sensation to feel like a third wheel at your own children's special events. Even when there's not a new significant other in the mix, attending your own children's events can feel a bit like a gauntlet of awkward exchanges that you (and the kids) must power through.

Do you sit with the other parent or not? Do you share a proud glance when your kid does well or keep your eyes facing forward? Who does the child hug first after the event without hurting the other parent's feelings? Or what if the other parent never shows up, either because they can't or choose not to, and you're left feeling like you have to compensate for that gap?

It seems like no one should have to go through this, and yet, so many families do. As much as I always want to ask God, "Why?" every time we go through this, I usually find myself landing on two truths:

1. God didn't put us here, but He will help us endure it.
2. Jesus said that we *will* have trouble in this world, but He followed it up with a call to courage and hope because He has overcome the world.

With Jesus, you too can overcome and rise above these potentially strained situations by making the experience as comfortable as possible for yourself and for your kids. Be gracious with the other parent. Invite other friends and family members to the events to reduce the awkwardness. And if the other parent brings a significant other to the event, remind yourself that no one can replace you in your kids' lives. You are a beloved parent, and no one else could ever take your place in the eyes of your kids.

How is Jesus inviting you to overcome strained family dynamics at your children's upcoming events? What mindset or action on your part will be necessary for you to rise above the situation?

Jesus, please help me release the humiliation and awkwardness I feel at my children's events because of our family situation. Give me confidence and resolve as I focus on making the situation as pleasant as possible for my children.

1 JOHN 5:4 · PSALM 20:10

28 following in faith

"As Jesus passed on from there, he saw a man named Matthew sitting at the customs post. He said to him, 'Follow me.' And he got up and followed him."

— MATTHEW 9:9

As single parents, you and I are often too busy to be as involved in church and in our community as we would like. Before I had kids, I helped lead RCIA classes and volunteered with the youth group, but once I was on my own with two kids, I no longer had the time or freedom to continue contributing at church in those capacities.

If I'm being honest, it wasn't just the lack of time that held me back. I also shied away from being involved in my church community because I felt like I wasn't worthy. I felt like I didn't fit and that my contribution would no longer be valued.

There may have been parishioners or parish staff that felt that way about me, but looking back, I believe this was more of a self-imposed limitation because I was embarrassed about my situation. I wish I had realized sooner that Jesus was calling me.

The story of Jesus calling Matthew has a special place in my heart. Matthew was a tax collector in Capernaum where Jesus lived and taught for a time. Tax collectors were considered sinners, outcasts, even traitors, and they were barred from religious worship too. Still, when Jesus passed by Matthew, He said, "Follow me."

Jesus didn't wait until Matthew got his act together or repented of his sins. He didn't wait for Matthew to ask. He met Matthew exactly where he was, at his job taking money from and oppressing God's people. And Jesus called him anyway.

The most beautiful part of the story is that Matthew didn't hesitate. He didn't pause to wonder why Jesus would choose him or waffle about whether or not he could give up his lifestyle. He simply got up from his post and followed Jesus. He left behind who he used to be and started over. He didn't know where Jesus would lead. He simply trusted and followed.

Jesus is ready to meet you exactly where you are too. It doesn't matter how you became a single parent or what mistakes you've made along the way as a single parent. Close your eyes and imagine Jesus standing in front of you. He looks directly at you, deep into your eyes as if peering directly into your soul, and with so much warmth and compassion says, "Follow me."

Jesus has chosen you. How is He calling you to follow Him today? Where does He need you to let go of the notion that you're not worthy or not welcomed so you can start living in community and serving His people?

Jesus, thank You for loving me just as I am and for meeting me exactly where I am. Give me the courage to set aside my limiting beliefs and to overcome the sense that I don't fit in. Show me how I should follow You.

LUKE 5:8-11 · JOHN 4:25-29

29 rest and relief

"Come to me, all you who labor and are burdened, and I will give you rest. Take my yoke upon you and learn from me, for I am meek and humble of heart; and you will find rest for yourselves. For my yoke is easy, and my burden light."

— MATTHEW 11:28-30

In the rare instances that I come across another single parent, it is refreshing and somehow calming to talk with another person who can truly relate to my situation and its challenges. There's one topic that always comes up—how very tired we are.

Let me be that friend for you today. I know you are exhausted, and some days you are so tired that your eyes physically hurt. I know this is hard, and it's overwhelming as the years of this workload and pace stretch out ahead of you. It feels like it will never end. You don't want to rush your children's childhood or wish it away, but you're just so very tired.

Your day starts early before the kids arise so you can begin preparations for the day. There are no mornings off because there's no other parent there to share in the chores or the driving.

You work hard all day to provide for your family. You're grateful for work, but oh, how you wish it did not take you away from your children for so much of the day. Somehow, you also squeeze in all of the doctor, dentist, and other appointments for your kids that have to occur during the workday too, even though it disrupts your work and causes you to fall behind.

Then, you come home to begin your other job of being a homemaker and parent. There's laundry, meal prep, and dishes, and if your kids are school age, there's homework, activities, and coaching your kids on how to manage social situations. Oh, and don't forget bath time, cleaning up the kitchen, and prepping for the next day. You cherish the precious moments of prayer time and cuddles with the kids, but it goes so fast. Then, you rest your eyes for a few hours and do it all again the next day.

I see you. And more importantly, Jesus sees you. Cry out to Him when you're weary. He is inviting you to let Him be your refuge and strength. He will not forsake you, even if you've been so busy that you haven't made time with Him a top priority lately.

This can be as simple as trying the "five-second rule" (and no it's not about how long food can be on the ground). When you are exhausted, take five seconds and say, "Jesus, I come to You. Give me rest." Say it as many times throughout the day as you need.

Where do you need Jesus to be your refuge and strength today? Have you asked Him for help? If not, why?

Jesus, I love my children and am blessed to be a parent, but my whole being is tired right now. As I cry out to You for refuge and strength, please remind me that You are by my side and swiftly answer my call for rest and relief.

JOSHUA 1:5 · 2 TIMOTHY 4:16-17

30 set free

"Free me from the net they have set for me, for you are my refuge."

— PSALM 31:5

I've often equated my experience as a single parent to that of a dog tethered to a tree who never knows how long the leash will be when it tries to run. It comes down to feeling stuck, and as you know, there are so many ways to feel stuck as a single parent.

Geographically, you may be tied to a place where you don't want to be due to the visitation agreement.

Physically and emotionally, you may be tied to that feeling of "surviving" instead of "thriving" because this journey is so taxing and consuming you feel like you can't find the time to enjoy simple pleasures.

You may have been so tired of being stuck that you finally decided to do something for yourself like following a new dream or achieving a new goal only to be yanked back by an unexpected delay or hardship.

I've experienced all three. Each time, it's as though I've run as far as the leash will allow me to go, and I can't quite get to where I want to be. I feel stuck.

We're called to have gratitude and joy in all circumstances, but occasionally, it's okay to say, "Set me free, Lord." It's okay to acknowledge the sensation of being stuck and to ask God for comfort as you settle into this place that isn't exactly where you want to be.

In what area of your life do you feel stuck? How might God be inviting you to stop straining to escape so you can make the most of where He's planted you? Or is He calling you to boldly ask Him to show you what you can do now to prepare for when the leash is finally untied?

Jesus, I want so badly to move on, but for some reason,
I am planted here, for now. Help me accept what I cannot currently
change, and help me to focus on and pursue the opportunities
You're giving me to grow, serve, and find joy right where I am.

PSALM 94:19 · ISAIAH 42:3

31 seen and heard

"Why, LORD, do you stand afar
and pay no heed in times of trouble?"

— PSALM 10:1

I've lost track of the number of times I've asked God why He's seemingly silent or still as I cry out to Him for help. At times, I find myself angrily demanding an answer. "I know You see me. I know You hear me. Why aren't You helping me?!"

I'm not sure what's worse—feeling like God doesn't see me or knowing that He does see me but seems to be choosing not to help me. The more certain I am that He sees me, the harder it is for me to understand why He seems to be ignoring my pleas for help.

If you've been there, you're in good company. Even King David sometimes felt like God was far away and not paying attention when he needed Him the most.

Keep reading Psalm 10. You'll find David lamenting the injustice of the situation and God's seeming inaction, but he doesn't stop there. He takes three important steps, and they are the same three steps that you and I need to take when we find ourselves in the same state of mind.

1. David calls out for action. "Rise up, LORD! God, lift up your hand! Do not forget the poor!"
2. David declares his faith. "To you the helpless can entrust their cause…"
3. David thanks God and praises Him as though the answer to his prayer has already come to pass. "The LORD is king forever…You listen, LORD, to the needs of the poor; you strengthen their heart and incline your ear. You win justice for the orphaned and oppressed…"

If you feel like God has abandoned you or is simply ignoring a particular prayer, try King David's formula. Call out to God, declare your faith, and praise Him as if He's already answered your prayer. This simple act may not immediately change your situation, but it might change the way you see the problem and close the gap between you and God.

Jesus, give me the faith and confidence of David to know that You are actively working to bring justice and resolution to my situation, even when it seems as though You are silent. I thank You ahead of time for hearing my cry and rescuing me.

2 KINGS 19:16 · PSALM 34:18

32 celebrate the wins

"May he remember your every offering, graciously accept your burnt offering, grant what is in your heart, fulfill your every plan."

— PSALM 20:4-5

Are you selling yourself short as a parent? If you aren't celebrating your wins, you should be.

It has been my prayer since the divorce that the kids will thrive despite our family situation. I'm sure you feel the same way about your kids. You know that your kids have had to overcome challenges that their peers in a two-parent home haven't shared, so the wins that your kids experience are especially sweet and leave you bursting with pride and thanksgiving.

Of course, we offer praise to God for every blessing He bestows on our children. We know that every good thing is a gift from Him and that it is through His grace that our kids learn and succeed. But I want to remind you that every win your kids experience is also due to the love and support you've poured into them.

Your work, sacrifice, and dedication to carrying out this epic responsibility of parenting alone is an offering, and through this offering, you've created an environment in which God can work powerfully in your life and in the lives of your kids.

You're also setting a beautiful example for your kids of what can be accomplished through sacrificial love and hard work. It is by God's grace that you do this, but you are choosing to do the work and put your kids first.

Whether your child is just taking his or her first steps, walking across a graduation stage, or reaching some other achievement in between, pause to acknowledge the role you played and celebrate YOUR win too.

God sees you and the work you have done to give your child this opportunity. He knows what you've given up and how much effort you poured into helping your child with this achievement. He's blessing your child's path, in part, because of you and through you.

Celebrate the wins. And when you do, while you're busy thanking God and congratulating your child, don't forget to acknowledge yourself too. You deserve it. Take a deep breath, smile, and whisper to yourself, "We did it!" Soak up the moment and let it carry you forward as you continue on this solo parenting journey.

Jesus, thank You for every blessing You bestow on my children and for every milestone and achievement You allow them to reach. Thank You for this win and for giving me the perseverance, strength, and resources to do my part in helping my child reach this goal.

JOEL 2:21 · DEUTERONOMY 10:21

33 releasing shame

"Do not fear, you shall not be put to shame; do not be discouraged, you shall not be disgraced. For the shame of your youth you shall forget, the reproach of your widowhood no longer remember."

— ISAIAH 54:4

In one of his YouTube videos*, Father Mike Schmitz offers a helpful explanation about the difference between guilt and shame. He says, "Guilt is failing to meet an objective standard of behavior—shame is failing in someone else's eyes." He tells the story of abused women in Africa who are welcomed back with great joy and love by their villages. In this way, the village lets them know they should feel no shame because no one views them any differently.

Single parents often carry a great deal of guilt and shame. We know to handle the guilt by confessing our sins, but the remedy for shame often seems elusive.

Sometimes, shame is triggered by an outside source, but more often than not, a single parent's shame begins internally. We have failed in our own eyes, and we can't seem to let it go.

How many times have you thought to yourself, "How could I have let this happen?" Or, maybe there is some other flavor of this question that's on repeat in your mind. You and I are our own worst critics, and because parenting goes on for decades, sometimes our shame does too.

Are you holding onto shame or regret about your situation?

God doesn't want you to stay in this place. He wants you to let it go, and this isn't just a suggestion.

In Isaiah 54, He tells you to forget the shame of your youth and to no longer remember. You may wonder how, but He has an answer for this too. Psalm 34 tells us, "Look to him and be radiant, and your faces may not blush for shame."

Maybe it's also time to follow the example of the African villagers and start speaking to yourself with joy and love instead of condemnation. Be gentle with yourself. You are more than your mistakes and regrets, and your children are proof of how God can bring beauty out of any situation.

Listen to how you speak to yourself today. Are you speaking to yourself with love, joy, and gentleness, or is your tone that of frustration, condemnation, and regret? How is God calling you to release any shame or regret that you're carrying and reframe how you view yourself?

*https://www.youtube.com/watch?v=CLTE_7NVIjY

Jesus, help me to see myself as You see me: radiant, forgiven, precious, and loved. Shut down the critical voice in my head and replace it with one of love, gentleness, and encouragement.

PSALM 34:6 · PSALM 31:2-3

34 **missed moments**

"The LORD is close to the brokenhearted, saves those whose spirit is crushed."

— PSALM 34:19

It's hard to come to terms with losing time with your children. That was what I dreaded and feared most during the divorce. It wasn't the moving out or closing a chapter. It was knowing that the process would end with a judge telling me that I would miss out on half of my kids' childhoods. It's utterly heartbreaking, and it's a pain that can only really be understood by other single parents who share custody.

You look on social media, and inevitably, you see parents in your circle of friends that comment about how hard it is to be away from their children briefly while they are away on a trip or the kids are at camp. When I see this, all I can think is, "That's nothing. Do they know how blessed they are to get all of the other days?"

As a single parent who shares custody, you miss so many firsts, memories, and experiences with your children. When the kids were little, this meant missing big firsts. As the kids have grown older, I've missed out on so many adventures with them. I wasn't there for big things like the first time they went skiing or camping. I've missed out on smaller but equally special things too, like the excitement and stories after school dances, because it wasn't my weekend with the kids.

Missing these moments, big or small, is soul-crushing to a parent. Whether this is due to a custody situation or a work obligation, the end result is the same. Your heart breaks, and you'd give anything to have these moments with your children.

Jesus knows your pain and longs to heal your broken heart. He knows the profound loss that you've experienced and how you have to experience it over and over again each time your kids head out on extended stays and new adventures with the other parent or other caregivers.

I have cried until I had no tears left over the time I've lost with my kids, and each time I find myself feeling crushed by this loss, my place of solace is at the foot of the Cross. It can be your place of solace too.

Next time you're feeling anguish over missed moments with your kids, remind yourself that your Savior knows soul-crushing loss too. He wants to meet you there amidst your pain and bind up your broken heart.

One way to do this is to find a crucifix in your home (or on your phone), put your hand over Jesus' feet, recall His tremendous suffering on the Cross, and ask Jesus to help you bear your suffering too. He longs to comfort you as you mourn these lost moments. You are not alone.

What firsts, memories, and moments with your children are you mourning because you missed them? How could you invite Jesus deeper into this pain with you so He can comfort your broken heart?

Jesus, my soul is crushed as I mourn all of the time I'm losing with my children due to visitation and work. Please meet me in my grief, fill me with Your peace, and bind up my broken heart.

ISAIAH 61:1-2 · MATTHEW 5:4

35 abundance

"A thief comes only to steal and slaughter and destroy; I came so that they might have life and have it more abundantly."

— JOHN 10:10

Have you ever read that verse and thought, "Maybe for other people, but not for me…"? As I look around at my single parent life, "abundant" isn't exactly the first word that comes to mind, but maybe it should be.

The meaning of this verse hangs on how you define "abundantly." It's tempting to adopt a worldly view of abundance and assume that it means an effortless overflow of happiness, success, money, power, perfect health, and fame or popularity. When I fall into the trap of comparing my life to others through this lens of worldly abundance, it is inevitable that I feel dissatisfied.

But Jesus' definition of abundant living is far different than that of the world. As Christians, true abundance is an overflow of the fruit of the Spirit, not worldly treasures. Galatians 5 tells us that the fruit of the Spirit is love, joy, peace, patience, kindness, generosity, faithfulness, gentleness, and self-control.

When you view your life through the lens of Jesus' definition of abundance, your level of gratitude will skyrocket.

- You may not have romantic love in your life right now, but you love your children in a deep and profound way and are loved by them in return.
- You may not always feel happy, but when you stay consistent with prayer, your soul will feel joyful even when your situation feels chaotic or unsteady.

- You may be running low on patience some days, but when you exercise self-control by pausing before you respond to your child and carefully choosing your words, you will notice that you both immediately feel more peace.

The more consciously you live the fruit of the Spirit, the more you will see the fruit of the Spirit reflected in your children. When this happens, you know what it really means to live abundantly.

I'll be honest. Some days, the kids and I nail it and experience the flow and peace of a "fruit-filled" day. But other days, we struggle to live even one fruit of the Spirit, often when we are at our most busy or tired. Luckily, God isn't asking us to be perfect, and each day is a fresh start.

How is God calling you to live more abundantly? Is there a particular fruit of the Spirit that you and the kids could focus on this week to more fully experience the abundant life Jesus wants for all of you?

Jesus, You've offered me an abundant life according to your standards, not the world's. Please help me and the kids to live "fruit-filled" lives filled with an overflow of love, joy, and peace that we can share with others.

ISAIAH 58:11 · 3 JOHN 1:2

36 something new

"Remember not the events of the past, the things of long ago consider not; See, I am doing something new! Now it springs forth, do you not perceive it? In the wilderness I make a way, in the wasteland, rivers."

— ISAIAH 43:18-19

Your life and mine now have two distinct periods—*before* becoming a single parent and *after*. If you're like me, you occasionally look back wistfully at who you were "before" and feel like many of your hopes, dreams, and even purpose have evaporated.

Scripture warns us of the dangers of looking back. In the Gospel of Luke, we're told to remember Lot's wife. This reference will take you all the way back to the Book of Genesis when Lot's wife was turned into a pillar of salt because she looked back longingly at what was she was meant to leave behind. Satan knows the easiest way to knock you off track for all that God has planned for you is to keep you tethered to your past and looking back.

When you dwell on the past, memories and emotions tend to bubble up to the surface and eat away at your sense of worth. There's a negative voice in your head that tries to tear you down with questions like, "How could you let this happen?" or statements like, "No one will ever want you now." Sometimes, that voice is so loud it's hard to hear anything else.

As you press forward into the unknown of this single parenting journey, God wants you to focus on the "after," not the "before." Like me, you probably feel so disoriented at times in this crazy experience of parenting alone that it's hard to clearly see what "after" is or could even be.

But my friend, God is doing something new. Aspects of your life may feel like a wasteland at the moment, but He will make a way.

No matter how you got here, you are on track for who He's calling you to be, and there are good things ahead. If you keep looking back, you will miss all that God has for you.

So make today the day. Let go of the past, face forward, hold your head high, and follow Him.

What part of your "before" is keeping you tethered to the past and looking backward? How is God inviting you to follow Him so He can do something new in your life?

Jesus, release me from any bonds that still hold me tethered to the "before." Show me the new and wonderful goodness that You have for me and my children in the "after" and keep our focus on You and moving forward.

GENESIS 19:17, 26 · LUKE 9:59-60

37 finding your place

"So he came to a town of Samaria called Sychar, near the plot of land that Jacob had given to his son Joseph. Jacob's well was there. Jesus, tired from his journey, sat down there at the well. It was about noon. A woman of Samaria came to draw water. Jesus said to her, 'Give me a drink.'"

— JOHN 4:5-7

At times, being a single parent feels like being banished. You might feel like you don't quite fit in with the single people, but you don't quite fit in with the married couples either. If we're being honest, the singles and married couples don't quite know what to do with us either. Single people can only listen to so many stories about your kids, and married people understandably seem to prefer hanging out with other married couples.

There are exceptions, of course, but this has been my general experience. I imagine you've been through this too. It leaves you longing for community and questioning if you'll ever fit in and find "your people" again.

Jesus answers that question with a resounding, "Yes!"

One of my favorite passages in the Bible is the story of the woman at the well. What I love most about this story is that Jesus sought this woman out even though she was an outcast (due to her marriage struggles and many mistakes). How do we know He sought her out? Because He arrived at noon.

During this time period, women traditionally went to the well together in the morning before it was hot. This woman, however, was there alone at mid-day because she was an outcast from society.

Jesus waited for her in the heat of the day, and through their exchange, she came to believe. This experience changed her in another significant way. She stopped viewing herself as an outcast and courageously stepped back into society to proclaim the good news. In fact, she is one of the very first people to directly evangelize about Jesus and the way He changed her life.

After their exchange, we read that the woman left her water jar and went into town saying, "'Come see a man who told me everything I have done.

Could he possibly be the Messiah?' They went out of the town and came to him." The story stops there, but I can only imagine how different her life was from that day forward.

I rediscovered my place and my people when I stopped viewing myself as an outcast and courageously stepped back into my church and friend communities looking for ways to serve. Jesus is calling you back to community and service too. By focusing on service to others, you will naturally find a renewed sense of purpose and belonging.

Are you putting limits on yourself by viewing yourself as an outcast? How is Jesus calling you to step back into your church and friend communities to serve a special purpose?

Jesus, change how I see myself and my role in the community around me. When I feel like I don't fit in, remind me that I belong to You, You have called me, and that I will once again find my place, my people, and my purpose if I focus on serving You.

LUKE 15:1-2 · MATTHEW 8:2-3

38 walking on water

"At once [Jesus] spoke to them, 'Take courage, it is I; do not be afraid.' Peter said to him in reply, 'Lord, if it is you, command me to come to you on the water.' He said, 'Come.' Peter got out of the boat and began to walk on the water toward Jesus. But when he saw how [strong] the wind was he became frightened; and, beginning to sink, he cried out, 'Lord, save me!' Immediately Jesus stretched out his hand and caught him, and said to him, 'O you of little faith, why did you doubt?'"

— MATTHEW 14:27-31

As a single parent, you will eventually hit a point where you feel like you're drowning. Maybe, you're there today. Something just feels like too much. It's dragging you down, and you feel unable to come up for air.

Lifeguards are taught to be very careful around a drowning person because, when you're drowning, your instinct is to pull others down in an effort to push yourself up. When this happens, the rescue is often unsuccessful because the lifeguard ends up in distress too.

The good news is that Jesus is your Lifeguard, and it's impossible to pull Him down.

You've probably seen one of the many illustrations of the moment when Jesus reaches down into the water to pull Peter up. Only moments before, Jesus had called Peter to step out of the boat in faith, and Peter had walked on water. He was fine until he took His eyes off Jesus, focused on the storm, became afraid, and began to sink.

The same thing happens in our lives. One minute, your problem seems manageable. With your eyes locked on Jesus, you're "walking on water" with full confidence that, together, you and Jesus have got this. The next minute, you become acutely aware of all that is swirling around you. You take your eyes off Jesus, and suddenly the problem seems bigger and out of control. And that's when you start to sink, fearing this problem will overtake you.

When this happens, you have two choices: drown or reach for your Lifeguard.

The most incredible and faith-inspiring part of the story of Jesus saving Peter from the water is that Jesus stretched out his hand and caught Peter. Peter didn't have to find the strength to grab onto Jesus. Jesus found him, grabbed his hand, and lifted him out of the raging waters.

And He's ready to do the same for you. Your Lifeguard is on duty, and He will not allow the raging waters to overtake you.

Identify what it is that's dragging you down and making you feel as though you're drowning. Now, look up and picture Jesus' hand reaching down to grab you. As His hand tightly wraps around yours and He lifts you up, what possible solutions can you see opening up for you, perhaps even beyond the obvious answer or miracle that you've been seeking?

Jesus, I am drowning right now, and I'm struggling to keep my eyes on You instead of the storm. Reach down and rescue me from the water that threatens to overtake me and bring me to safety.

2 SAMUEL 22:17-18 · PSALM 69:16-19

39 wonderfully made

"You formed my inmost being; you knit me in my mother's womb. I praise you, because I am wonderfully made; wonderful are your works! My very self you know. My bones are not hidden from you, when I was being made in secret, fashioned in the depths of the earth."

— PSALM 139:13-15

As a mom and adamantly pro-life Catholic, I've read Psalm 139 many times. I delighted in this verse both times that I was pregnant as I thought of how God knew my children from the moment of their conception (and even before) and carefully knit them together as they grew.

Your children are wonderfully made by God, and you have likely made a conscious effort to communicate this to them. You relay this message by sharing Scripture and your faith with them, but you also relay this message by how you love and care for them. You know them, sometimes better than they know themselves, and love them accordingly.

If that is how much you love your own children, imagine how much more God loves you.

On days when you feel lost or forgotten, remind yourself that this verse in Psalm 139 applies to you too.

- You are wonderfully made. No matter what has gone on in your life, you are wonderfully made and loved.
- God knows your very self. He knit you together and knows you more intimately than you know yourself.
- He will never forget you. You are engraved upon the palms of His hands.
- He knew you and gave you your name before you were even born.

Could you ever forget your own children? Of course not.

If you and I, as flawed people, can't forget our children, how much more impossible would it be for your heavenly Father whose love is so vast and so wide, who knows you so intimately, to ever forget YOU?

How does your situation look different if you base your outlook on the assumption that God loves you and has never forgotten you?

Jesus, thank You for the gift of my children and for so carefully crafting their bodies and souls. When I feel forgotten as I wait for an answer to prayer, please remind me that I was fearfully and wonderfully made by You too and that You gaze upon me with an even more deep and profound love than I feel for my own children.

ISAIAH 49:15-16 · ISAIAH 49:1

40 finding joy

"A joyful heart is the health of the body, but a depressed spirit dries up the bones."

— PROVERBS 17:22

Have you ever wondered if you're depressed? (This could mean experiencing clinical depression diagnosed by a professional or just generally feeling discouraged or feeling low in spirit for more than just a day or two.)

If so, you are not alone. When you look at the statistics from various studies of single parents, you'll find that anywhere from 20 to 30 percent of single parents are battling depression.

The Mayo Clinics' list of the symptoms of depression* reads like a laundry list of emotions that single parents experience regularly. Is it any great surprise then that you and I might wonder from time to time if we are depressed?

Because the symptoms are familiar feelings, depression can sneak up on us and wreak havoc on our lives. In Proverbs 17, God tells us that "a depressed spirit dries up the bones." This means that depression steals your strength and life.

If you have felt or are feeling depressed, I pray that you know there is no shame in experiencing depression, and there is help available. You can seek help from family, friends, your church, a counselor, and your doctor. You can also call 911 or a hotline if you need immediate help. You don't have to battle this alone.

Most importantly, you can seek help from God to overcome depression and low moods. In Ezekiel 37, we see how God breathed life back into dry bones. No matter how down you feel or how long you've felt this way, there is hope. God wants to breathe life back into you.

Proverbs 17 doesn't just warn us about the effects of depression. It also tells us the antidote to depression—a joyful heart. This refers to true joy, not the passing feeling of happiness. True joy is not based on what's happening around you. Rather, it's based on your belief in Jesus and in His gift of salvation.

I didn't fully grasp that until I hit a point of experiencing depression. During that difficult time, I realized that I could still bask in the joy of knowing that, no matter what I had lost, I still had Jesus. This spiritual joy allowed me to discern the best path for me to get help processing all of the other emotions, and for me, that path was working with a counselor.

If you're feeling depressed now, how might God be calling you to address those feelings and reconnect with your joy? If you're in a joyful place today, take note of how you're holding onto your joy despite the challenges you face each day, and apply this on days when you might be feeling low.

*https://www.mayoclinic.org/diseases-conditions/depression/symptoms-causes/syc-20356007

Jesus, please protect my mind, body, and soul from depression and fill my heart with the true joy of knowing You and accepting the gift of salvation that You offer. If I ever do experience depression, remind me that I do not have to battle it alone, and guide me to help and healing.

PSALM 126:5 · ISAIAH 35:10

41 amazing possibilities

"We know that all things work for good for those who love God, who are called according to his purpose."

— ROMANS 8:28

I wouldn't trade my kids for anything, but my days as a single parent leave little free time for the other things that used to feed my soul. At times, I feel a bit lost and rudderless in this life I never anticipated, and that feeling is often accompanied by a nagging sense that I'm missing out on what God originally had planned for me.

Do you feel a sense of purpose and direction, or are you feeling a bit lost and rudderless?

Thankfully, our loving Father works ALL things for good, even when it feels like we are off track. Yes, even this heartbreaking and exhausting chapter can yield good. Often, this happens in unexpected ways.

Before I became a single parent, I had a life coaching business and dreamt of speaking and writing books. When I became a single parent, I no longer had the freedom or the confidence to continue the life coaching business, and the dream of writing a book evaporated along with the business. This left me feeling like I had missed out on part of God's purpose for my life.

I made peace with the fact that, for a season, I was called to focus solely on being a caretaker and breadwinner, but the sense that I was called to more lingered. For over a decade, I prayed and asked God what else I was supposed to do. The idea that I should write kept popping up, but I had no idea what to write. One day, I just knew what God wanted me to do, and I reached out to Dynamic Catholic with an idea about generating content for single parents. That call ultimately led to this book!

Even if you've felt a bit lost and aimless for an extended period of time, don't give up. Perhaps, it's not God's time for your next pursuit, but He definitely has a purpose for you.

What possibilities would open up before you if you could embrace the notion that God has a special purpose for you BECAUSE of what you've been through, not in spite of it?

Jesus, please use this chapter of my life to mold me into who You want me to be. Show me how to use what I've been through to live out the plan You have for me and remind me that You have a special purpose for me because of my journey as a single parent, not in spite of it.

EPHESIANS 2:10 · PSALM 139:16-17

42 choices we make

"Trust in the LORD with all your heart, on your own intelligence do not rely; In all your ways be mindful of him, and he will make straight your paths."

— PROVERBS 3:6

Can you think of a time when your feelings led you away from what you knew God would have wanted you to do? I can almost see you cringing and shaking your head "Yes" because I am right there with you!

"Trust in the LORD" seems like such a straightforward instruction, but God didn't stop there because He knows what we do. Powerful emotions hit us, and suddenly, it's a free-for-all. You and I sometimes follow those emotions on a whim or, worse, talk our way around a situation and rationalize a decision that we know, deep down, is not what is best for us.

So, God continues in Proverbs 3 and adds, "…on your own intelligence do not rely."

Just in case we didn't catch it earlier, God kicks the message up a notch in Proverbs 28 when He says, "Those who trust in themselves are fools, but those who walk in wisdom are safe."

Yowza. There's no room for confusion there. If you want to make wise choices, you need to make your decisions based on your trust in God and His wisdom, not on your feelings and rationalizations. Feelings can be so unreliable and are often fleeting. You might feel strongly about something today but feel completely different tomorrow.

You might be mad at your boss today and feel like resigning, but tomorrow, you wake up and feel really thankful you still have your job. Imagine the regret if you had actually resigned.

Tonight, you might feel desperate for some physical or emotional attention, but tomorrow, you wake up and feel really thankful you went to your own home instead of to someone else's house. Imagine the regret if you had given into that temptation. The examples are endless.

The moral of the story is: You can't rely on your feelings, but you can rely on God's love and wisdom.

There are three questions that you can ask yourself when you feel emotions tugging you down a path:

- Does this choice align with God's Word and bring me closer to God?
- Is this the decision I would make if Jesus were standing right here with me?
- When I stand before God for judgment upon my death, will I be proud of this choice?

Any one of those questions can help you reel in the feelings so God can make straight your path.

Jesus, in moments when I am filled with powerful emotions, teach me to pause and open my eyes to the path You have for me.

LAMENTATIONS 3:25-26 · PROVERBS 28:26

---

43 God's presence

"Trust God at all times, my people!
Pour out your hearts to God our refuge!"

— PSALM 62:9

Imagine going fifty years feeling completely cut off from God but choosing to serve Him anyway.

That's exactly what Saint Teresa of Calcutta did. You may know her better as Mother Teresa, and for fifty years of her life as a nun serving the poorest of the poor in India, she experienced doubt, despair, and loneliness because she could not feel God's presence. (If you're curious to learn more, check out the movie about Mother Teresa called *No Greater Love*.)

Other saints have experienced this too. In the sixteenth century, Saint John of the Cross labeled this experience as the "dark night of the soul."

While you may not have gone through a full "dark night of the soul," you have inevitably noticed that some days God feels closer than others. I wouldn't wish this on anyone, but I find it somehow comforting that even the holiest people among us sometimes feel like God is far away.

It can be tempting to give in to the doubt, despair, or loneliness that you feel when God seems far away. The only way to combat this temptation is to ground yourself in this truth:

God is with you whether you "feel" Him or not.

The further away God feels, the more important it becomes to exercise your trust in Him.

- Keep talking to Him—every day.
- Voice your trust in Him—out loud and on repeat.
- Continue to act and serve as though He's right there with you—because He is.

When God feels far away, it's because I've moved away from Him, not the other way around, and I know it's time to examine my life, figure out what's causing the perceived gap, and address it. The next time God feels far away from you, I'd invite you to do the same.

Where have you stepped away from God?

Jesus, my feelings are tempting me to believe that You have abandoned me, but I know You are here with me. Shine a light on any area of my life that is separating me from You, show me how to fix it, and fill me with assurance of Your loving presence.

ISAIAH 26:4 · PSALM 91:2

44 **persevering in prayer**

"Rejoice in hope, endure in affliction, persevere in prayer."

— ROMANS 12:12

During difficult moments in this journey, it is tempting to turn my back on God. After all, it sometimes feels like He's turned His back on me.

Satan works hard to draw us away from God. One of his favorite tactics is to convince us that God has turned away from us when we experience a long-term affliction. Whether your affliction is mental, emotional, physical, spiritual, or financial, it may be so intense that holding onto your faith requires resolute determination that is only possible when you persevere in prayer. It is when we are most weary and feeling a bit abandoned that we need to double down on our prayer and hope in God.

Scripture is full of examples on how to apply this underrated virtue. Paul persevered in prayer for years from prison. Abraham and Sarah persevered in prayer for a child for decades. Jesus gave us the story of the persistent widow in Luke 18 to drive home the importance of persevering in prayer.

In my own attempts to persevere in faith, I've experienced a lot of variation in my path back to realizing that God has never left my side. Sometimes, I need a good workout or a good cry while I belt out worship music until I feel myself let God back in. Other times, I need to focus on serving others instead of wallowing in my self-pity, or I need to spend time in Adoration where I can always speak to Jesus heart-to-heart until I feel my peace return.

Persevering in prayer looks different for each person. Some people connect with God in nature. Some people connect with God at church. Some people connect with God when they are alone, and others feel most connected to God when they worship and serve Him with other people.

When your affliction drags on and leaves you feeling as though God has turned his back on you, do you tend to turn toward God or away from God? How could you crank up your efforts to persevere in prayer?

Jesus, I'm exhausted and overwhelmed, and it feels like You have forgotten me. Please fill me with peace and faith that You are by my side and help me persevere in prayer, especially on the days when I do not feel like it.

LUKE 18:1 · JAMES 5:13

45 **beauty for ashes**

"To announce a year of favor from the LORD and a day of vindication by our God; To comfort all who mourn; To place on those who mourn in Zion a diadem instead of ashes; To give them oil of gladness instead of mourning, a glorious mantle instead of a faint spirit."

— ISAIAH 61:2-3

Becoming a single parent changed everything. No matter what happened next, I knew there was no going back to what I had always pictured, which was all of us living together under one roof and building a beautiful life together.

The day that I drove away for the last time from the home that I shared with my husband, I felt deep despair, and the hopes and dreams that I'd had for my life and my kids' lives disappeared into a steaming pile of ashes.

When something is burned to ash, it is burned beyond recognition or repair. It can never be made whole again as it once was, but the ashes can be used to bring forth something good. And in Scripture, God promises to do just that.

Have you ever heard the phrase "beauty for ashes"? It comes from Isaiah 61:3 where God promises to give beauty (or a beautiful diadem or crown) in place of your ashes. He promises that your mourning will be turned to gladness.

In the Old Testament, people put ashes on their heads to represent their internal grief, shame, disgrace, disappointment, regret, and sorrow, hence the exchange of ashes for a crown. Sometimes, their sadness and loss were so great that they literally sat on a pile of ashes.

Do you ever look at aspects of your life and feel like you too are sitting on a pile of ashes because of the losses you've experienced? If you do, don't despair. We have a God who can work wonders with the ashes in our lives.

There is good yet to come in your life, even if it doesn't seem like it some days. God can and will bring something beautiful from this difficult situation if you cooperate with Him to discover what that beauty might be.

How is God calling you to use what you've been through to bring beauty into your life or the lives of others? What beautiful gifts has He given you, besides your children, that you would have missed if life had gone as planned?

Jesus, in my darkest moments, it's so hard to see how You will bring beauty from the ashes in my life. Please help me hand over my ashes to You by accepting what is, so I can be ready to experience the beauty and joy that are to come.

GENESIS 50:20 · REVELATION 21:4

46 **forgiven and free**

"Again he bent down and wrote on the ground. And in response, they went away one by one, beginning with the elders. So he was left alone with the woman before him. Then Jesus straightened up and said to her, 'Woman, where are they? Has no one condemned you?' She replied, 'No one, sir.' Then Jesus said, 'Neither do I condemn you. Go, [and] from now on do not sin any more.'"

— JOHN 8:8-11

At times, being a single parent can feel like a punishment. During a particularly rough stretch, like when I have the flu but have to get out of bed anyway and take the kids to school because there's no one else to do it, the thought creeps in that my situation may somehow be a punishment for past sins.

Have you ever felt like you were being punished as you face the challenges of being a single parent?

Please let me assure you that no matter how you became a single parent, Jesus loves you deeply, and He is not punishing you for some unforgivable sin. Satan uses our regret and shame to make us feel as though we deserve to be punished, but that's not how Jesus works.

Rather, Jesus is inviting you to seek His forgiveness. If you've already sought forgiveness through confession, Jesus has already forgiven you. It's time to give yourself permission to release the regret and shame, and it's time to ask God for the grace to stop condemning yourself. After all, Jesus has already told you that He does not condemn you.

If you haven't confessed your sins yet, I guarantee you will feel your burden lighten (spiritually, mentally, emotionally, and even physically) if you confess your sins and ask Jesus for forgiveness. If appropriate, you will feel the burden lighten further if you apologize and make amends to any person that you hurt. Jesus is not using the difficulties in your life to punish you. He's inviting you to live in the freedom of His forgiveness.

Walking in the light of forgiveness will allow you to again view the opportunity to be a parent as a blessing, not a punishment, regardless of any ups or downs you experience.

What regret or shame are you holding onto that He wants to liberate you from?

What regret or shame are you holding onto even though Jesus has already forgiven you?

Jesus, I know my situation is not a punishment, but sometimes it feels that way. Please help me to confess any sin I'm holding onto that makes me feel like I am less than who You created me to be. Allow me to live in the light of Your forgiveness and to remember that You do not condemn me.

HEBREWS 4:16 · PSALM 32:5

47 claim victory

"Now I know the LORD gives victory to his anointed. He will answer him from the holy heavens with a strong arm that brings victory."

— PSALM 20:7

It's a memory that will haunt me forever.

Leisure time is rare and precious in my world, and the kids and I had just arrived at the park. The kids took off running toward the playground, and almost immediately, my daughter tripped and fell very hard on the cement, scraping her hands and knees badly.

As she sat there sobbing on the ground, my immediate reaction was to shake my head and yell at her for not watching where she was going. I didn't rush to hold her or wipe away her tears. I yelled at her out of frustration that we'd have to go home and would lose our precious playtime.

I felt instant regret for what I said, but it was too late to take it back. I looked into her tearful, scared eyes and knew that my words had done more damage than the fall. In that moment, I felt like I had completely failed my daughter and as a parent.

Do you have your own parenting fail that lingers in the back of your mind? On days when you know you haven't been at your best as a parent, you may be tempted to believe you're failing as a parent altogether, but that simply is not true.

A bad moment does not make you a bad parent any more than a temper tantrum makes your child a bad child. Read that again. You are human, and you're going to make mistakes. That doesn't define you as a parent.

The very fact that you are turning to God during this challenging time in your life shows how much you care about being a good parent. It's time to remember that you are anointed and that God has promised you victory. That includes victory as a parent.

Rather than beating yourself up for a moment of less-than-stellar parenting, focus your attention on taking a positive next step toward a parenting victory. Pause and ask God what your children need most from you today. Laughter? Compassion? Wisdom? Help? An apology? A hug?

God will help you discern the right answer so you can act on it. The beauty of this parenting journey is that you can claim victory over a day, an hour, or even a moment. If you stumble, forgive yourself and let it go because, by God's grace, you can still win the day!

What victory will you claim for yourself and your kids today?

Jesus, reach down from Heaven and bring victory into my parenting approach. Wipe away my regret and disappointment over the moments when I was not at my best as a parent and show me how to more perfectly love my children today.

DEUTERONOMY 20:4 · PSALM 149:4

48 **faith over fear**

"Do not fear: I am with you; do not be anxious:
I am your God. I will strengthen you, I will help you,
I will uphold you with my victorious right hand."

— ISAIAH 41:10

Do you know what one of the most frequently repeated phrases is in Scripture? "Do not be afraid."

As single parents, worry can become a regular part of our daily existence. God knew how often you would cry out, "Lord, I am afraid," and He knew how much you would fret about your kids, your finances, your health, your work, and every other aspect of your life. So, He repeated those comforting words over and over.

"Do not be afraid."

Easier said than done, right? Well, He knew you'd say that too.

In Isaiah 41, God gives you a litany of promises to assure you that you can let go of your fear and trust Him:

- The Creator of the moon, sun, and stars is with YOU even when you feel like He is far away.
- God delights in you and is ready to listen anytime you're ready to talk.
- When you feel weary with worry, you can turn to God in worship, prayer, fasting, and adoration, and He will give you strength.
- It's not a question of "if" God will help you but "when."
- God might lift you over a problem so you can avoid it altogether, or He might walk through the trial with you. Either way, you can be sure that He is holding onto you.

What fear is gnawing at you today? How is God inviting you to trust Him more deeply as He whispers to you, "Do not be afraid"?

Jesus, I know I need to trust You in the moments when I am filled with fear. Please strengthen me, hold me close, and give me steadfast faith that You will help me.

PSALM 46:2-3 · PSALM 23:4

49 **resentment**

"Do everything without grumbling or questioning..."

— PHILIPPIANS 2:14

A wave of resentment hit me during preparations for our early Thanksgiving dinner this year. I don't resent the kids, of course, but there are days when I feel resentful that I am parenting and providing alone.

During the week of Thanksgiving, the kids already had plans with friends that couldn't be rescheduled, and I was left to shop, cook, and wash dishes by myself. When the kids arrived home, they found me in the kitchen angrily mumbling and grumbling under my breath. I was so frustrated that I actually threatened to cancel Thanksgiving next year if they couldn't be bothered to stay home and help. Yikes! It was not one of my finer moments.

Later, after I had apologized to the kids and calmed down, I had to laugh at the irony. I'd been mumbling and grumbling during my Thanksgiving prep, instead of being, well, thankful.

As a fellow single parent, I imagine you've hit your breaking point and done your share of mumbling and grumbling too. Clearly, you're not alone!

Thankfully, God has a lot of experience dealing with the ingratitude of His people. In Numbers 14, the Israelites grumble and complain to Moses and Aaron about being stuck in the wilderness instead of being thankful that God had just freed them from slavery. If you jump to verse 11, you can see God's response.

"And the LORD said to Moses: 'How long will this people spurn me? How long will they not trust me, despite all the signs I have performed among them?'"

I imagine God's response to our grumbling is the same as when He responded to the Israelites.

In Philippians 2, God tells us to do everything without grumbling or questioning so we can be blameless and shine like lights in this world. The only way to achieve this is to stay in a place of gratitude and trust instead of letting the resentment and frustration take over.

In what area of your life do you feel frustration or resentment building? I challenge you to pause now to find at least one thing to be grateful for in that same area of your life. When you do, you might be surprised to find that you can almost immediately think of more reasons to be grateful. Once you shift your focus, it's easier to see your blessings.

How could you integrate this practice into your daily life to minimize resentment, reduce complaining, foster gratitude, and express trust in God, even in your most frustrating moments?

Jesus, in the moments when I am most tempted to grumble and question, please remind me of how You have blessed me in the past and are blessing me now. Fill me with gratitude and remind me to trust and praise You at all times.

NUMBERS 14:2, 11 · 1 PETER 4:9

50 your parenting partner

"...that he may grant you in accord with the riches of his glory to be strengthened with power through his Spirit in the inner self..."

— EPHESIANS 3:16

Reflect for a moment on the fact that the Holy Spirt, the third person of the Holy Trinity, dwells in you, and that because of this, you are strengthened with power that comes to you through God himself. It's quite astounding when you really think about it.

Consider the times when you felt called to pay for a stranger's meal, make a clothing donation, or take a different route home than usual. Those gut feelings were actually nudges from the Holy Spirit helping you understand and (hopefully) follow God's will. The more you call upon the Holy Spirit, the easier it becomes to:

- Sense and follow those nudges
- Allow the power of the Holy Spirit to work in your life

I believe the Holy Spirit empowers single parents in a special way. Most parents have a spouse that they can talk to and bounce ideas off of as they figure out how to handle the adventures of parenting. You and I don't have that partner, and it can feel like a tremendous responsibility to figure it all out alone.

But we aren't actually alone. God is closer to you than you can comprehend through the Holy Spirit that dwells in you, and the Holy Spirit is ready to empower you as your partner on this parenting adventure.

One area that can be particularly challenging to navigate without a spouse is disciplining your child. There's no taking turns with the other parent to be the "bad guy" who doles out consequences. It's all on you and it can wear you down unless you invite the Holy Spirit into the process.

When I invite the Holy Spirit into the discipline process, there's a palpable shift in the whole experience for me and for my child. I can feel the Holy Spirit guide the conversation and help me display compassion, listen to understand, offer a thoughtful explanation, share words of wisdom, and choose a meaningful consequence. My child also tends to respond more respectfully and constructively than when I try to go at it alone.

The Holy Spirit is with you too and ready to pour power and strength into you. When was the last time you prayed specifically to the Holy Spirit to ask for help disciplining your child or for guidance, strength, protection, or wisdom in other areas of your life? Where could you use the Holy Spirit's help today?

Jesus, I am filled with gratitude that You sent the Holy Spirit to dwell in me and be with me as I navigate this parenting journey without a partner. Please help me hear the Holy Spirit and fill me with Your strength and power to handle the challenges of parenting with grace and love.

COLOSSIANS 1:9, 11 · 1 CORINTHIANS 12:7

51 **divine mercy**

"As far as the east is from the west, so far has he removed our sins from us. As a father has compassion on his children, so the LORD has compassion on those who fear him."

— PSALM 103:12-13

Worship music is my go-to solution when the kids and I need an instant boost in our mood and energy. My playlists are full of songs from many wonderful Christian artists. One of my favorite contemporary Christian groups is Casting Crowns, and they have a song called "East to West" that beautifully describes the promise of Psalm 103.

The beautiful lyrics remind me that, through Jesus' sacrifice on the Cross, He offers us love, salvation, and *mercy*. His forgiveness changes us. Our sins are literally wiped away. We aren't meant to carry that shame and regret with us after we've asked for forgiveness.

I don't know about you, but the mistakes of my past haunt me sometimes, especially when the consequences of those mistakes carry into my present and future and affect my kids. When I confess my sins, I know I have been forgiven. But because the consequences continue, it feels like I can't really leave the sin behind.

And worse, sometimes I repeat the sin and wonder, "What will God (and the priest) think when I confess this sin again? Will God be willing to forgive me for this again?"

Hebrews 4 answers those questions as God reminds us that our high priest, Jesus, is able to sympathize with our weaknesses because He too was tested. No matter how big or how frequent your sin, you can approach His mercy in the Sacrament of Reconciliation, and if you come before Him with true contrition, He will forgive you. And when He forgives, He casts your sin as far as the east is from the west.

When you need a reminder about how vast God's mercy is, try saying the closing prayer for the Divine Mercy Chaplet: "Eternal God, in whom mercy is endless and the treasury of compassion—inexhaustible, look kindly upon us and increase Your mercy in us, that in difficult moments we might not despair nor become despondent, but with great confidence submit ourselves to Your holy will, which is love and mercy itself."

If, in His compassion, God can forgive you so completely, shouldn't you forgive yourself too? Identify the sin that you just can't seem to let go. How can you begin the process of forgiving yourself today?

Jesus, after I have come to You in confession for forgiveness, fill me with Your peace and help me to know that I am truly forgiven. Give me the compassion to forgive myself, amend my life, and move forward in the freedom of Your forgiveness.

PHILIPPIANS 3:13-14 · HEBREWS 4:15-16

52 **restored**

"When the LORD restored the captives of Zion, we thought we were dreaming. Then our mouths were filled with laughter; our tongues sang for joy. Then it was said among the nations, 'The LORD had done great things for them.'"

— PSALM 126:1-2

It may not seem like it right now, but there will come a day when God restores you. I don't know which area of your life needs to be restored at the moment, but I'm sure it wouldn't take you long to pinpoint one (or more) places where you could use some restoration.

After my divorce, my greatest fear was that my children's lives would be ruined from growing up in a broken family. It felt like we might not ever be okay and had lost our opportunity to flourish.

While our situation has certainly taken a toll on the kids and me, we're not down and out. God has restored laughter and joy to our home. He has allowed the kids to thrive under less-than-ideal circumstances. He has restored my hope for our family by showing me that this divorce will not define us nor our futures.

Restoration does not always mean replacing exactly what you lost or getting back what you once had. Rather, God rebuilds and restores you based on His will and knowledge of what you truly need. And sometimes, He restores you with even more than you had in the first place.

Receiving God's restoration requires us to trust despite our circumstances. If we strive to be content and to wait with prayer and patience after a loss, He will move to help us rebuild.

In what area of your life (or your children's lives) are you in need of God's restoration?

I believe it's only a matter of time before you see God moving in your life to bring that restoration. Do you?

Jesus, I praise You and thank You for all that we do have. You know even better than I do what area(s) of my life and my children's lives need to be restored, and I pray that You will one day restore us according to Your will.

JEREMIAH 30:17-18 · ISAIAH 61:7

53 **be still**

"And your ears shall hear a word behind you: 'This is the way; walk in it,' when you would turn to the right or the left."

— ISAIAH 30:21

What do you do when you hear a soft, seemingly distant noise behind you? You pause, get quiet, and strain to hear it again, right?

We know God spoke to Elijah in a still, small voice, and He often speaks to us that way too. It's interesting that Isaiah says you will hear God's word "behind you." It makes me think of a parent following closely behind a child on a walk and offering words of wisdom and advice about how to stay safe and enjoy the adventure. I'm also reminded that, when I want to hear God, I probably need to pause my activity, get quiet, and actively listen for God to speak to me, so I don't miss it.

I've found that I hear God most clearly in the quiet of the early morning before the kids wake up, at Adoration, and at the beach as I close my eyes and listen to the waves roll in and out. The common denominator here is that I hear God the best when I am still and quiet. We all need stillness and quiet in order to hear the voice of God.

As a single parent, it is especially difficult to find time to be still and quiet. When your children are little, they require round-the-clock care, and when they are older, the pace and frequency of activities soar off the charts. No matter the children's age, quiet time is a luxury for a parent.

I've learned that I need to consistently make a conscious effort to carve out quiet time with God. It may mean rising a little earlier or staying up a little later, but the benefits far outweigh the lost sleep. It may mean asking a family member to stay with the kids for a bit so I can sneak away for a walk or to my favorite bench at the lake. If the kids are safely contained, it may simply mean staying in the bathroom for an extra couple of minutes to take a mini-break from the commotion and try to hear God more clearly.

Sometimes, when you can't get away, you just have to pause right where you are and listen. Assuming the kids are safe and can be without you for a moment, try it now.

Pause where you are and get still. Now, close your eyes, take a deep breath in and out, and *listen*.

What is God whispering to you today?

Jesus, help me create opportunities to be still and quiet. Attune my ears to Your voice and allow me to clearly hear as You speak to me.

JOHN 16:13 · PSALM 85:9

54 coping with holidays

"Peter began to say to him, 'We have given up everything and followed you.' Jesus said, 'Amen, I say to you, there is no one who has given up house or brothers or sisters or mother or father or children or lands for my sake and for the sake of the gospel who will not receive a hundred times more now in this present age...'"

— MARK 10:28-30

Mother's Day and Father's Day can be difficult days for a variety of reasons, but these days come with a special mix of emotions for single parents. One emotion that is consistent, regardless of whether it's "your" holiday or the other parent's holiday, is the feeling of being forgotten.

On "your" holiday, there is no other parent there to plan and coordinate the celebration or recognize the blood, sweat, and tears that you pour into raising your children. If your kids are like mine, they do their best to celebrate with you, perhaps with homemade cards and gifts or breakfast in bed. It's lovely, but it's not the same has having the other parent acknowledge you and thank you for all that you do for the kids.

Of course, this holiday falls on a Sunday. On "your" holiday, you might take the kids to church where you can't help but watch the "normal families" where there's a spouse actively working to make it a special day for the other parent.

Wouldn't it be amazing if your parish held a Mother's Day Brunch or Father's Day Brunch for single parents, so you could feel like someone sees you too? Like someone recognizes the sacrifices that you make every day to carry this load of filling the role of both parents?

My friend, please know that Jesus sees you. He sees your love and sacrifices for your children even when no one else does, including when you sit at church alone feeling heartbroken and tearful on the other parent's holiday. Through these sacrifices, you are storing up treasures in Heaven, but that doesn't always relieve the pain here on Earth.

I have a feeling that Mother Mary empathizes with single parents, and I imagine she has a special place in her heart for single parents. After all, at some point, it seems she was likely a single parent herself. We don't know exactly when or where Joseph passed away, but it's unlikely that Jesus would have entrusted His Mother to John's care from the Cross if Joseph were still alive.

Mary knows. And if she knows, imagine how intimately aware Jesus is too. Your reward for all that you have sacrificed will come in time. Until then, you can have peace in knowing Jesus sees you and is with you.

Jesus, I am so deeply grateful for my children, and while I don't do the work of parenting because I expect a reward, it brings me peace to know You see me. Please remind me that You are always with me, and I am not alone.

MATTHEW 6:6; 19-20 · MATTHEW 25:23

55 **contentment**

"Why does the way of the wicked prosper, why do all the treacherous live in contentment?"

— JEREMIAH 12:1

It is mind-boggling to me that so many people who clearly do not prioritize following Jesus seem to enjoy such prosperity while I work so hard to follow Jesus but only scrape by. Where is the justice in that? If you have found yourself wondering the same thing, it looks like we are in good company, as this question shows up in the Book of Jeremiah and in other places in the Bible too.

I usually try to keep my temptation to compare my life and finances to others in check, but last week, I had a moment of weakness. While I was sitting at a traffic light, I saw a car pull up in the lane next to me. This car easily cost more than my house. Guess what the license plate read? "NO*GOD"

I could be wrong, but based on other things I observed, including the profanity-filled music pouring out of the car, I don't think the driver was trying to communicate "Know God."

After I picked my chin up from the dashboard, I thought, "God, I'm a single mom working so hard to follow You. I desperately need a new car and have no idea how I'll afford one. I've prayed, but I'm still not sure how I will fit a new car into the budget. Why would you give such an extravagant vehicle to someone who does not seem to love You, or even know You, but not provide a vehicle for me?"

I knew it was wrong to envy the other driver's comfortable lifestyle and to be so presumptuous about how and when God should answer my prayers, but the unfairness of it was hard to swallow.

How often do you look around and experience the same type of envy and the same kinds of questions?

You and I are not alone in our desire for things to be easier and more comfortable, but as children of God, we are called to rise above this desire and to instead seek contentment with what we have.

It doesn't mean we can't ask God for good things. It just means we need to accept His will and timing in how He chooses to provide for our needs. We also need to ground ourselves in gratitude for what He has already given to us.

In what area(s) do you feel envious of others or feel like you deserve more because you do your best to faithfully follow God? Now that you're consciously aware of this, how might God be inviting you to let go of the envy and seek contentment?

Jesus, I confess that I am envious of others more than I should be. Please forgive my lack of gratitude and help me to find contentment with and appreciation for all that You have generously provided for me and my children.

PSALM 73:12-14 · JOB 21:13-14

56 God whisperers

"This poor one cried out and the LORD heard, and from all his distress he saved him."

— PSALM 34:7

When you talk to a person, it's pretty easy to tell if the person is actively listening to you or not, especially when you're sharing a problem you're facing or asking for help. If that person is making eye direct contact, asking questions, expressing interest and empathy, and avoiding distractions while you speak, you know he or she is actively listening to you.

But when you communicate with God, there's no physical "proof" that He's listening because the verbal and non-verbal indicators of active listening aren't there. You have faith that He hears you and will answer in His own way, but when you go for a long stretch without obvious intervention or answer from the Lord, you may start to worry that God is ignoring you or that He simply does not hear you.

I've been there. I once prayed for an entire year about a particular intention with seemingly no movement or response from God. It left me feeling unheard and worried that maybe God just couldn't hear me, or worse was ignoring me.

God's word is filled with promises that He is with you and hears you, and His word is filled with examples of proof that these promises are true. But on my toughest days during this year of prayer, the promises didn't feel like enough. I needed more, and God delivered.

God reminded me that He often speaks to us through other people. There are two ladies in my life who are my "God Whisperers." Anytime I share my struggles with them, they drop everything, lean in, and truly listen. They respond to me with such Godly wisdom and encouragement that I know God is speaking to me through them. I feel heard, and I know I am loved. Through their words and support, God reassures me that He is actively listening to me and that He will, in time, answer me. I'm not sure I would have made it through that year of waiting for God to move without them.

The next time you wonder if God even hears you, try turning to His Word for reassurance that He hears you. If you need more, try to summon the courage to be vulnerable and share your problems, fears, and needs with trusted family and friends. Allow God to remind you that He is actively listening to you through the responses from those people.

Who are (or who could be) the "God Whisperers" in your life? In what other ways does God show you that He is actively listening to you even if He is not immediately answering your prayer?

Jesus, please help me notice all of the ways that You show me You're actively listening when I cry out to You, especially when Your answer to my prayer does not come right away. Fill me with peace and help me to trust as I wait for You to answer.

PSALM 143:7 · PSALM 40:2

57 amazed by you

"I have the strength for everything through him who empowers me."

— PHILIPPIANS 4:13

Whether you're a fan of war movies like *Saving Private Ryan* or *Top Gun*, or you've just simply watched the news lately, you've inevitably seen examples of how war can change people.

Being a single parent may not be as extreme as fighting in a war, but it's an intense, gritty, surreal experience that leaves you feeling like you fought a battle. Until you've lived it, it's hard to comprehend the tireless work, endless pressure, and utter exhaustion that accompanies raising children alone. No matter how much time you spend as a single parent, you're likely to come out on the other side with "war stories," forever changed.

Through the haze of this long battle, you're so focused on surviving that sometimes you don't even notice how valiantly you're fighting to simultaneously provide for, protect, nurture, teach, guide, and pray over your children without the help of a partner. You're simply doing what needs to be done, much like a soldier on the battlefield who runs toward the danger instead of away from it. It's all just part of a day's work.

When I see my college roommate, she always acknowledges the magnitude of what it is to parent alone, and at some point during our time together, she usually says, "Kelly, I don't know how you do it."

I've always been grateful to her for saying this. It feels good to hear that from someone who is a wife and a mother. It's nice to feel like someone notices, and it's nice to have validation that this really is an unbelievably hard job that is often more intense and demanding than the typical parenting experience. Every parent works hard, but parenting alone requires you to level up.

In case no one has told you lately, you are AMAZING! It takes courage and determination to do what you do every day. It also takes strength.

I know that some days strength is harder to come by. On those days, it's time to remind yourself that Jesus has promised to empower you with strength for everything. When you are weak, you are actually strong, if you let Jesus do what He does best, because Christ can work through you beyond what you could ever accomplish by yourself.

When this battle is done, you're going to look back with pride in what you were able to accomplish. Until then, know that you've got this because, with Jesus, *all* things are possible, even single parenting.

When is the last time you paused to acknowledge or celebrate your determination and hard work so far? Where do you particularly need to call on the strength of Jesus to help you power though today?

Jesus, on my own, I might not make it, but with You,
I know all things are possible.

2 CORINTHIANS 12:10 · MARK 10:27

---

58 **bold action**

"Therefore, since we have such hope, we act very boldly..."

— 2 CORINTHIANS 3:12

Nothing knocks us off our pedestals faster than making a doozy of a mistake. Before I became a single parent, I was a confident person who felt sure she could "win" in most situations, from winning arguments to achieving goals. In my arrogance, I would sometimes judge others and condescendingly say, "Choices we make," when commenting on someone's unfortunate outcome. In my mind, it was black and white. They should have thought it through and chosen differently if they wanted a better outcome.

Then came my big mistake. I married the wrong person, which ultimately led to my becoming a single parent. Boy did it sting when someone close to me ridiculed me and my situation by sarcastically saying, "Choices we make, right?"

Those words haunted me for years and destroyed my confidence, but I had to admit that the person was right. Against the recommendation of everyone close to me, which I believe was God's way of trying to clearly show me the right path, I had chosen poorly, and the consequences would last a lifetime. After that, I questioned whether I could ever regain the confidence to trust my own choices and pursue new goals in the future.

Perhaps your path to single parenthood or some other decision in your past has left you contemplating the same thing. After making a big mistake, it's natural to become more hesitant about taking chances and making future decisions. You might feel like it's safer to stay stagnant rather than risk another mistake, but that's not where God wants you to stay.

God is calling you to learn from your mistake and move on. He wants you to trust Him and trust yourself to act boldly when He calls you to take action.

If you need a little confidence boost in the department of decision making, I'd highly recommend Father Mike Schmitz's book, *How to Make Great Decisions*. In this short read, you'll find practical steps for knowing when God is speaking and for making wise decisions, so when you do finally decide what step to take, you can feel empowered to move forward with confidence.

What will you do the next time God calls you to move forward toward a new goal or action that He wants you to take? Will you hesitate and hide because of past mistakes, or will you act boldly?

It's your choice to make.

If God is calling you to move now, what's the first step you could take toward making a wise decision and acting boldly in faith, hope, and trust in God?

Jesus, please help me to learn from past mistakes and to let them go so I can move boldly when You call me to action. Give me the confidence to trust that You will guide my steps and choices when I seek to do Your will.

PROVERBS 28:1 · ROMANS 8:31

59 God's providence

"My God will fully supply whatever you need, in accord with his glorious riches in Christ Jesus."

— PHILIPPIANS 4:19

Aside from reading Scripture, one of the best ways to renew your faith in God's providence is to simply look back at your life and recall all the ways He's provided for you in the past. It's especially inspiring to remember the ways God showed up in your life even bigger than you dared hope He would.

As I look back at ways in which God has provided even more than my children and I needed, the memory of my children's first full-time babysitter comes to mind. For many reasons, putting my children in full-time childcare was difficult for me. It's just not how I imagined they would grow up.

Through my tears, I prayed that God would help us find the right childcare provider, and He answered mightily. By following God's lead, I not only found a babysitter, but I found someone who fit our needs perfectly. She was our very own "Mary Poppins." She knew exactly what each of us needed, including me, and she cared so perfectly for us. I'm still convinced she was an angel that God put in our path to help us through this difficult transition.

You may not need childcare at the moment, but chances are, you have a need of some kind that you're hoping and praying God will fill. How confident are you that God will fully supply what you need?

What is one example of how God has generously and bountifully provided for you and your children in the *past* that would help shore up your faith that He will meet the need that you have *now*?

Jesus, I trust that You know exactly what the kids and I need and that You will meet our needs in Your way and in Your time. Please give me peace in the waiting and give me wisdom to follow where You lead me.

EPHESIANS 3:20-21 · 2 CORINTHIANS 9:8

60 **reading and reflection**

"For whatever was written previously was written for our instruction, that by endurance and by the encouragement of the scriptures we might have hope."

— ROMANS 15:4

When you sit down to pray, do you ever find your mind wandering? If you're like me, you have the best intentions to engage with God, but suddenly items from your To-Do list start intruding on the conversation.

I love you, Lord. (What should I make for dinner tonight?)

I praise you, Lord. (Did I remember to charge my phone?)

One way to focus your mind on God is to pray the Scriptures, which is also known as Lectio Divina. The Catechism describes Lectio Divina as "the prayerful reflection over biblical and other spiritual texts." In this approach, we meditate on what God is saying to us specifically through His Holy Word.

I've found this approach to reading and reflecting on the Bible to be incredibly powerful during my lengthy journey as a single parent. At church, we tend to read Scripture from the perspective of how God is calling us to carry His message and mercy out into the world. Through Lectio Divina, on the other hand, I hear and feel God speaking to me on a personal level about His love and mercy for me as an individual.

My entire outlook on life changes when I practice Lectio Divina consistently. It has drastically reshaped how I believe God sees me (especially as a parent), what I believe is possible for my future and the kids' futures, and how I approach God for guidance in resolving difficulties that come my way.

Ready to give it a try? The Lectio Divina prayer includes four simple steps:

1. Slowly read a Scripture passage. For this example, read 1 Kings 17:12-15.
2. Reread the passage and meditate on what you just read. Notice what part of the message resonates with you and connects with your thoughts and feelings that day.

3. Pray and speak with God about your insights from the reading. Ask God to clearly show you what He's saying to you through this passage.
4. Rest in God's presence. Be still and linger in this place of connection with God. Soak up His love.

That's it. If you gave it a try, how do you feel? How could you integrate this into prayer time with your children?

Tip: I'm often so delighted by what God has revealed to me that I record it in my journal so I can deepen my reflection and preserve it to enjoy again at a future date.

Jesus, I believe You want to speak into my life. Teach me to listen to Your Word in the Scriptures and hear the message You have for me today.

PSALM 119:105 · 2 TIMOTHY 3:16-17

---

61 cherished

"Because you are precious in my eyes and honored, and I love you, I give people in return for you and nations in exchange for your life."

— ISAIAH 43:4

How long has it been since you felt loved and cherished?

I know that's a hard question. It's one of those questions that's usually easier for me to avoid than face head-on. If I don't think about it, I'm okay, but if I dwell on it for too long, the sadness and tears start to well up. Sound familiar?

Being a single parent can be hard on your sense of self-worth for many reasons. From your path to becoming a single parent to your day-to-day life as a single parent, there's often a running theme of rejection that can leave you feeling "less than," disregarded, and discarded.

How you've experienced rejection is unique to you, but I want you to know that you're not alone. I know what it is to feel an ache in your heart as you long to be cherished. I also know what it is to battle that voice in your head that sometimes tells you that you're not worthy of being cherished.

Today, God wants you to know that you ARE worthy, and you ARE cherished. Any notion to the contrary is a lie from the enemy.

Here are just a few of the ways God demonstrates how much He cherishes you:

- He loves you beyond measure exactly as you are.
- He knows you, and you are precious in His eyes.
- He wrote an epic love letter to you, the Bible, so you could know Him and His love for you.
- He lavishes you with gifts and talents and longs to help you be the best-version-of-yourself.
- He chooses to be with you always, and His greatest joy is to spend time with you and listen to you.
- He wants to share your load and lift your spirits when you feel low.
- He rejoices with gladness over you and sings joyfully because of you.
- He is always willing to forgive you when you haven't been at your best.
- He sacrificed His only Son to save you and show you His unconditional, everlasting love.

(Isn't it interesting that this basically describes what you would be looking for in an ideal partner in life too?)

Now, close your eyes and bask in that love for a moment. When you have a few minutes, write those statements out as first-person declarations. For example, the first bullet point would become, "God loves me beyond measure exactly as I am." Do this for the whole list. Then, reread this list daily to remind yourself that, no matter what else happens in your day, you are absolutely worthy, loved, and cherished.

Jesus, please flood my heart, body, mind, and soul with Your love. Help me to know beyond any doubt that I am cherished and loved by You, always.

ZEPHANIAH 3:16-17 · LUKE 15:20-24

62 refusing to worry

"Peace I leave with you; my peace I give to you. Not as the world gives do I give it to you. Do not let your hearts be troubled or afraid."

— JOHN 14:27

There is something you could do today that would change EVERYTHING but cost NOTHING.

That thing would be to *refuse to worry*.

Peace can be hard to come by for single parents. You and I can always seem to find something to worry about. Money, home maintenance, work, childcare, how the kids are doing in school, whether or not the tooth fairy will remember to come, the kids' safety, the long-term effects on the kids from growing up in a single parent home. The list could go on.

I'm sure you have a list of worries too. In fact, there are probably days when worry consumes you. I experience the same thing. But Jesus is always calling us to have peace.

More than once, Jesus said to His disciples, "Peace be with you."

At the Last Supper, in His last moments with the disciples before the Passion unfolded, Jesus made a point of telling them, "Do not let your hearts be troubled or afraid."

Let me throw a bold question out to you: How would your life be different if you consciously chose not to allow anything to trouble you and instead relied on your faith in Jesus and in His promises of peace, provision, and protection?

It's hard to give up a bad habit, like worrying, cold-turkey, and honestly, it may not be realistic to give up worrying altogether. We're human, and the temptation to worry will always be there. If you're not in a place to give it up altogether, you can still reduce the amount of time and energy you spend worrying.

Which particular worry could you hand over to Jesus today in exchange for His peace? When the temptation to pick that worry back up creeps in, how will you remind yourself that this particular worry isn't yours to carry today?

Jesus, worry consumes too much of my time and steals joy and peace from the kids and me. Show me how to release my worries to you and allow You to pour Your peace into my life so I can come to honestly say, "My heart is not troubled or afraid."

COLOSSIANS 3:15 · PHILIPPIANS 4:6-7

63 **running the race**

"Therefore, since we are surrounded by so great a cloud of witnesses, let us rid ourselves of every burden and sin that clings to us and persevere in running the race that lies before us while keeping our eyes fixed on Jesus, the leader and perfecter of faith..."

— HEBREWS 12:1-2

Whether you're in the early years of parenting and dealing with diapers and sleep training or you're in the teen years and dealing with hormone changes and driver training, the parenting victory of seeing your child reach adulthood can feel far away.

The single parenting race toward this victory is unique in that you're not just anticipating your child turning eighteen or graduating high school. You're probably also looking forward to gaining back a bit of your freedom from some of the unpleasant constraints you're experiencing now. If you're divorced, that list might include a forced visitation schedule, geographic restrictions on where you can live, or stress-inducing financial entanglements with the other parent.

If you're wondering how to power through until that day comes, God offers great advice:

- Keep your eyes fixed on Jesus.
- Persevere in running the race that lies before you.
- Run so as to win.

In the Bible, God offers these instructions within the context of pursuing salvation, but you can certainly apply these tips to the single parenting race too. Keep your eyes fixed on Jesus instead of dwelling on frustration with all of the complications in your situation. Run the race that lies before you without dwelling on the past and looking back. You can't change what happened. All you can do is move forward with Jesus. And last, but not least, run so as to WIN. You can do this. It's hard, but with God's help, you can make it to the finish line.

It may not always feel like it, but there is light at the end of the tunnel. One day, this race to the end of the restrictions and complications will reach a finish line. And when it does, I pray that you and I will both be able to say, "I have competed well; I have finished the race; I have kept the faith."

Which of God's three tips for running a successful race would be most helpful to you in your single parenting race this week, and how will you put that tip into action?

Looking long-term, which freedom do you think you will enjoy the most when your child becomes an adult, and you're no longer bound by the constraints of your single parenting race?

Jesus, on the days when I worry that I don't have the strength or endurance to finish the single parenting race, please remind me to follow Your strategies for not just finishing this race but winning it. Help me to hold onto my faith that I can compete well with You by my side.

1 CORINTHIANS 9:24 · 2 TIMOTHY 4:7

---

64 **connection**

"And then a leper approached, did him homage, and said, 'Lord, if you wish, you can make me clean.' He stretched out his hand, touched him, and said, 'I will do it. Be made clean.' His leprosy was cleansed immediately."

— MATTHEW 8:2-3

How brave and desperate was the leper as he approached Jesus to ask for healing? Because leprosy was such a highly contagious skin disease, anyone with leprosy was considered "ritually unclean" and excluded from community life and worship. The man was an outcast and had no one. Yet, he approached Jesus to ask for healing, and Jesus, in His love and mercy, healed the man. Next, Jesus tells him to go to the priest so the priest could see that he was clean and allow him back into the community.

Jesus wants this for you too.

Being a single parent can sometimes make you feel like you need to step back from your social circles, community, or even your church. You might withdraw because you feel like you don't fit in, you're embarrassed by your situation, you feel like you're no longer welcome, you're too busy, you don't have childcare, or some combination of all of these reasons. Whatever the reasons, this withdrawal can lead to isolation, and the isolation can make you feel like an outcast, whether you are or not.

Over the years, I've learned that I need to ignore that fear of not fitting in and just go for it when I'm invited to an event. A few weeks ago, I was invited to a party with several friends I hadn't seen in a long time. When the day arrived, I was exhausted from work and had a million things to do. It was so tempting to stay home, but I went anyway. And I was so glad I did!

It felt good to connect, and I was reminded that fitting in is about so much more than whether or not I have a spouse. We laughed about getting older and about the ups and downs of raising teens. We shared stories of our kids and reminisced about when they were little. I was reminded of how comforting and uplifting it is to be part of a group, and I received more hugs than I'd had in a long time. It was good for my soul.

If you've been in a season of isolation or feeling like an outcast, Jesus is reaching out with healing and reassurance. He is calling you back into community. You're not "unclean" because you're a single parent. You belong, and your friends, community, and church need you.

Give it a try. Next time you're invited to an event with friends, commit to yourself that you'll go. You might have to force yourself to go and work through the sense of dread as the start time approaches. But once you are there, you will likely find that connecting with friends sparks joy and a sense of belonging, and that this time will feed your soul.

Jesus, please free me from my limiting belief that I don't fit in. Give me a sense of belonging and help me find opportunities to connect with my friends, community, and church.

HEBREWS 10:24-25 · PROVERBS 17:17

65 intentional parenting

"From the fruit of their mouths people have their fill of good, and the works of their hands come back upon them."

— PROVERBS 12:14

The other parent's presence, or lack thereof, inevitably rocks the boat some days, and this can leave you with a serious need to vent your frustrations, perhaps rightfully so. I experience this more frequently than I'd like to admit.

It can be incredibly tempting to voice my annoyance in front of my kids. Sometimes, this happens accidentally in the heat of the moment, and sometimes, deep down, I'm tempted to make a comment on purpose because I selfishly want the kids to view me as "right" and the other parent as "wrong." Whether I've only thought it or actually let the words slip out, I feel convicted when this happens. Have you been there too?

A friend of mine once told me that the best gift his mother ever gave him was that she did not speak negatively about his dad even though they were divorced. Because of this, my friend was not predisposed to a tainted view of his dad, and he was able to form his own opinion of his dad over time based on his own unique experiences and observations.

That stuck with me, and I believe that one of the greatest gifts I've given to my children is to do my best to offer the same opportunity to them. You're in a position to offer that gift to your children too.

It's natural and healthy to process your feelings about how the boat may have been rocked on a given day, but the key is to consciously choose a time when the kids are away to privately work through those feelings with a counselor, a trusted friend, or even in confession. Over the years, I've also found that the less time I spend dwelling on it mentally and vocally, the faster the frustration fades.

It takes practice and discipline to manage the emotions and to be intentional about what you communicate in front of your kids. When you need motivation for self-control in this area, take some time to read the Book of Proverbs. God repeatedly reminds us of the power of our words and calls us to remember that they create very real rewards and consequences in our lives.

Are you ready to give your kids the gift of not speaking negatively about the other parent or other important people in their lives? If not, what's holding you back?

Jesus, I know my kids' perception of the other parent is important to their mental, emotional, and spiritual well-being. Guard my thoughts and words so I can allow them to develop their own opinions of the other parent based on their unique experiences and observations.

PROVERBS 16:23-24 · PROVERBS 13:3

66 anxiety antidote

"Some rely on chariots, others on horses, but we on the name of the LORD our God. They collapse and fall, but we stand strong and firm."

— PSALM 20:8-9

The moment finally arrives. I lay my weary head on the pillow for what feels like the first moment of quiet in my day. And then it begins: the rapid-fire, intrusive, anxious thoughts that keep me up at night even when I'm exhausted.

Tomorrow, I need to schedule the orthodontist appointment. Did I tell the sitter about the schedule change? Ugh, I forgot to put the trash out today. Why is the car making that noise? What if God doesn't answer my prayer (in the way that I hoped)?

Your list might be different, but I bet you have one too.

Some nights, you fall right to sleep, and other nights it feels impossible to shut down the swirl of thoughts racing through your mind. When this happens, it's so tempting to reach for your phone or the TV remote. But guess what? The blue light from screens actually makes it take even longer to fall asleep. The screen might distract you, but it doesn't actually ease your anxiety.

This anxiety doesn't come from God, but by His grace, you can call on the name of Jesus to combat the anxious thoughts. You can also apply a quick, scientifically-proven method to trigger your mind and body to calm down. It's called "The Physiological Sigh," and it's one of the ways that Navy Seals swiftly calm themselves on the battlefield. This breathing method begins to calm my anxiety almost immediately.

You can transform the breathing process into a prayer by adding in the name of Jesus.

The steps are simple:

1. Inhale two times in a row
   (one longer breath in followed by a short second breath in).
2. Speak the name of Jesus as you exhale slowly.
3. Repeat as needed until you feel your peace return.

In James 4:7, we read, "So submit yourselves to God. Resist the devil, and he will flee from you." When you call on the name of Jesus, you submit yourself to Him, and the enemy who is trying to steal your peace will depart.

So, next time you can't sleep because of anxious thoughts, just breathe in, breathe in again, breathe out with Jesus, and repeat. It won't take long before you are relaxed and ready to sleep.

Jesus, I call on Your holy name for protection and peace. Thank You for the gift of Your holy name to free me from anxiety and enable me to find rest.

JOHN 14:13-14 · PSALM 124:8

67 awaiting rescue

"...We were utterly weighed down beyond our strength, so that we despaired even of life. Indeed, we had accepted within ourselves the sentence of death, that we might trust not in ourselves but in God who raises the dead. He rescued us from such great danger of death, and he will continue to rescue us; in him we have put our hope that he will also rescue us again..."

— 2 CORINTHIANS 1:8-10

From the time you were young, you were likely taught to take your troubles to God and have faith that He would help you fix your problem. Where does that leave you when you've exhausted every option, and God still doesn't swoop in to rescue you?

A disastrous outcome can leave you questioning God's good plans for you, His faithfulness, and even His existence altogether. I found myself with these same questions as I faced a particularly devastating loss. I prayed for over a year for help and restoration, but nothing in my situation changed. I struggled to reconcile my absolute faith and trust in God's love for me with His absolute silence in this area of my life that I had covered in prayer for so long.

I couldn't help but think of Mary and Martha. Their brother, Lazarus, was sick, so they sent word to Jesus. When Jesus arrived, Lazarus had been dead for four days, and Martha, and later Mary, couldn't help but say, "Lord, if you had been here, my brother would not have died."

You and I do the same thing when we fall into despair over a seemingly unanswered prayer. We cry out, "Lord, if You had been here, this wouldn't have happened."

In the story, Jesus does, indeed, rescue Lazarus, but it happens in the most unexpected way. Instead of saving Lazarus from dying, Jesus raises him from the dead. When you're in crisis, God does eventually act on your behalf. It may not be when you wanted it to happen or in the way that you prayed it would happen, but He will always rescue you, again and again.

I'm still praying for help and restoration, but I see God moving and bringing me to life in new ways through this trial. The waiting is different when you trust in God's sovereignty over your life. Your perspective shifts from anxiety and fear to curious anticipation. It becomes easier to endure in hope and easier to remember that this is temporary. Of course, this doesn't mean that the anxiety doesn't creep in, but when it does, you're able to shut it down by focusing on God's truth—rescue is coming. It's only a matter of time.

It's tempting to think it would be easier if prayer worked like a gumball machine. I pray, and then God immediately pops out a reward by answering my prayer exactly how I think it should be answered. But you and I know we are called to a more mature faith. Mature faith means believing God is in control and has a plan even when we are suffering.

Where have you prayed for rescue from God that hasn't come—yet? How is God using this situation to strengthen your faith or bring something new and beautiful into your life?

Jesus, I begged You for help, but You didn't answer in the way that I had hoped. Help me see how You are using this profound loss to bring me closer to You and shape me into the person that You need me to be.

JOHN 11:1-45 · PSALM 107:19-20

68 **building their faith**

"Fathers, do not provoke your children to anger, but bring them up with the training and instruction of the Lord."

— EPHESIANS 6:4

When you had your children baptized, you made a promise to raise them in the "practice of the faith." (If you haven't had your children baptized, I'd encourage you to reach out to your local parish for information on how to obtain this Sacrament for your children). This promise made at baptism is a lifelong commitment, but it is during their childhood when you lay this important foundation.

It can be a challenge for single parents to ensure their children receive proper faith formation. The kids may be gone for half the weekends with the other parent, which is further complicated if the other parent does not share your faith or is unwilling to be a part of the kids' faith formation. Even if the kids are home, it can be difficult to get to faith formation classes due to work schedules, transportation issues, or other valid conflicts.

This challenge really boils down to one question: Could there be anything more rewarding than seeing your children actively live out their faith as they love and serve the Lord? I'd argue that this singular outcome would bring you and your children greater joy than any other successes they experience because the impact would be eternal.

When you look at it from that long-term perspective, it clarifies how crucial it is to make faith formation a priority. Whether you're just getting started or are looking to ramp up your children's faith formation, here are a few steps you can take at home and in partnership with your parish to raise your kids in the Catholic faith:

At home, you can:

- Integrate age-appropriate, faith-based, apologetics literature into your reading time with your kids (apologetics = how to explain and defend the faith by being able to explain why we believe what we believe).
- Let your kids see you live your faith at home and in your community.

At your parish, you can:

- Speak with your children's faith formation coordinator about your situation so they understand why your children may be absent more frequently than other kids in the class.
- Request a copy of the materials that you can take home and use for make-up lessons when your kids have to miss class.

I found that my parish was extremely willing to work with me once they understood our situation, and I'm hopeful your parish will be too. How faithful have you been to your promise to raise your children in the faith? Are there areas in which you could make faith formation a bigger focus for you and your children?

Jesus, my greatest joy will be to know that my children are walking with You and living the truth of their faith. Guide me as I raise them, and show me the steps I should take to raise them in the faith despite the challenges of our family situation.

3 JOHN 1:4 · PROVERBS 23:24

69 **fill your cup**

"Just so, your light must shine before others, that they may see your good deeds and glorify your heavenly Father."

— MATTHEW 5:16

You, my friend, are doing an amazing job with your kids. Truly, you are doing a great job. I wish I could tell you this in person because these are important words for every single parent to hear.

If you read those words and your thoughts immediately jumped to mistakes you've made along the way, I want you to shut that voice of condemnation down. When it comes to parenting, it's about effort and progress, not perfection, and you pour so much effort into caring for your children.

You can be sure you're doing an amazing job with your kids despite any mistakes you've made along the way because your efforts line up with God's word:

- You love your children intensely.
- Whatever you do for them, you do from the heart, as for the Lord.
- Through all of your love and sacrifice, your light shines before your kids who see your good deeds and glorify God for the gift of having you as their parent.

Yes, even on the days when you drive your children crazy with chores and high expectations for their behavior and effort, they praise God for YOU.

If your relationship with your children currently feels a bit strained or even off the rails completely, you can take comfort in the fact that you're laying a solid foundation for your children, even if they aren't exactly singing your praises at the moment. Just keep loving your kids, showing them how deeply you care about them, and allowing them to see your joy in being their parent (particularly on the tough days). In time, you'll see how well that foundation served your children, and you'll likely find that your relationship with them is back on track.

What are you most proud of in regard to how you parent?

Today, make a special effort to tell each of your children three things that you love about them and why.

Then, ask your children to share three things that they love about you.

This simple exercise will fill your cup and theirs with extra love and joy that will last well beyond today, and it will let your light shine even brighter to glorify God.

Jesus, thank You for the people in my life who fill my cup by letting me know that I'm doing a great job with my kids. When no one notices, please fill me with peace that You see me and are pleased with my efforts to love my children well and to glorify You.

COLOSSIANS 3:23 · 1 PETER 4:8

---

70 **forgive them**

"Put on then, as God's chosen ones, holy and beloved, heartfelt compassion, kindness, humility, gentleness, and patience, bearing with one another and forgiving one another, if one has a grievance against another; as the Lord has forgiven you, so must you also do."

— COLOSSIANS 3:12-13

God's call to forgive doesn't seem like a monumental challenge until I'm face-to-face with a situation that feels unforgiveable, particularly one that involves the other parent. No matter how amicable I try to act toward my kids' dad, there's always an underlying tension and history of hurt that make it difficult to see the good and forgive, especially in a situation that feels unforgiveable. When this happens, I show up to my conversations with God armed with a litany of excuses for why it's just too hard to forgive this time.

And then, I read a passage like Colossians 3:12-13, and I'm convicted to my core that God's call to be compassionate, kind, humble, gentle, patient, and forgiving applies most especially to disagreements with my kids' dad. I have to remind myself that my willingness to forgive does not make the other person right, and then, I grit my teeth and do my best to offer forgiveness and compassion, whether I feel like it or not.

Finding forgiveness can take time and resolve to achieve, but it can be achieved. One of the biggest mistakes we make when it comes to forgiveness is treating it like a feeling. We think to ourselves, "Someday I will wake up and my heart will be ready." But forgiveness isn't a feeling. It's a choice.

Our faith and obedience to God are put to the test when we're called to live with love even though we don't feel like it. We're not just called to forgive. We're called to forgive the way God has forgiven us. It's one thing to read God's word and claim we believe. It's quite another to actually live out the difficult teachings and rise to the occasion as God's chosen, holy, and beloved.

You may be facing your own seemingly unforgiveable situation with the other parent or another family member. Are you ready to choose forgiveness, or are you holding tightly to your litany of reasons why this situation is unforgiveable? What steps could you take toward forgiveness, even if you don't feel like forgiving the person?

Jesus, help me to choose forgiveness, kindness, and compassion regardless of how I feel. Let Your words, "Blessed are the merciful," echo in my mind and drive me to live with love, especially with those that I struggle the most to love.

MARK 11:25 · MATTHEW 5:7

71 overcoming bitterness

"Trust in the LORD and do good that you may dwell in the land and live secure. Take delight in the Lord, and He will give you what your heart desires."

— PSALM 37:3-4

For about five years of my career, I taught high school business, technology, and career planning courses. The first thing I bought for my classroom when I became a teacher was vinyl lettering that read, "Wake up every morning with the thought that something wonderful is going to happen." I chose this decoration to inspire hope and joy in my classroom full of teenagers, but I think I needed that reminder as much as they did.

Before my divorce, I did wake up every morning with the thought that something wonderful was going to happen, and it usually did. Once I became a single parent, particularly as I tackled the challenges of the first year of teaching, bitterness eventually replaced that joyful anticipation.

I loved my students and the sense that I was making a difference in my professional life. But on a personal level, I felt disillusioned and bitter. I struggled to wake up each day anticipating good things, and I wasted more time than I'd like to admit feeling sorry for myself because life looked so different than I had imagined.

Maybe your situation has also left you feeling bitter and disillusioned or feeling sorry for yourself. If so, I'd like to offer you a formula from Psalm 37 for how to rediscover and hold onto your hope and joy even though life looks so different than what you had imagined.

First, hold on to your trust in God, even if it feels like you're barely hanging on some days. Trust that His plan for you is still good even if it is different than you imagined.

Second, when you feel the bitterness start to bubble up, look for an opportunity to do something nice for someone else. This can be a simple gesture like sending an encouraging text to a friend that you know is going through a difficult time. Service and kindness are the antidotes to bitterness.

Third, delight in the big and little blessings from God that pop up each day and give thanks. Be intentional about noticing every blessing God sends your way, especially the simple blessings like the comfort of a cup of warm coffee or tea in your hand or the sound of your child's laughter. You can't be grateful and bitter at the same time.

Psalm 37 says that, if you do these things, you will be secure, and God will give you what your heart desires. Does that mean your every wish will come true? Maybe not, since the desires of our hearts don't always align with God's will for us. But what it does mean is that you can trust that God has good plans for you, and there is good reason for you to wake each morning with the thought that something wonderful is going to happen.

How is God calling you to let go of bitterness and uplift others as you wait for His timing and plans for you?

Jesus, help me to use my time and energy to do good for others rather than dwelling in bitterness. Fill me with joyful anticipation of the good things that You have planned for me.

ISAIAH 30:18 · PSALM 33:20-21

72 enough

"Such confidence we have through Christ toward God. Not that of ourselves we are qualified to take credit for anything as coming from us; rather, our qualification comes from God..."

— 2 CORINTHIANS 3:4-5

There is a universal truth about being a single parent. We all feel like we're not doing enough. There is only so much time in the day, and you and I hold ourselves to impossible standards, often forgetting that this parenting job would be a lot for two people, let alone just one.

I don't know about you, but I'm particularly hard on myself when it comes to how I care for the kids. For example, I strive to make healthy, homecooked meals, but some nights, the best I can do is a frozen, precooked meal-in-a-bag from the grocery store. Instead of focusing on the fact that I made sure my kids had a hot meal even though I had to work late, all I can think about is how I let them down by feeding them a meal full of preservatives.

I do the same thing when I beat myself up for not spending enough time with the kids, not keeping the house clean enough, being too stressed and not laughing enough with the kids, and not having enough resources to provide everything they might need or want.

I bet you do the same thing.

There is a sign in my kitchen, and I want to share the message with you. It reads: "You do enough. You have enough. You are enough."

That is God's message to you today. YOU do enough. YOU have enough. And YOU are enough.

This is not by your own merit but by the grace of God. He promised you that if you remain in Him, He will remain in you and allow you to produce much fruit. And that's exactly what you are doing as you work tirelessly to care for and provide for your children in every way. Much like with an apricot tree or an apple tree, it may be years before you see the fruits of your labor, but if you generously sow the seeds now, you will eventually see the fruit sprout and grow as your children become the men and women they were meant to be.

It's time to cut yourself a break and pat yourself on the back. It's time to notice the good and the sacrifice in your efforts instead of focusing on how you wish you could have done it better. It's time to remember that you are God's handiwork, and He created you to be more than enough for all that He has called you to do.

In Him, you are enough.

In what way are you struggling to feel like enough? How is God inviting you to acknowledge that you do enough, you have enough, and you are enough?

Jesus, I end most days feeling like I didn't do enough. Please renew my perspective so that I can more clearly see all of the ways that You help me to do, have, and be enough for my children.

JOHN 15:5 · EPHESIANS 2:10

73 calm in a crisis

"For he shall never be shaken; the righteous shall be remembered forever. He shall not fear an ill report; his heart is steadfast, trusting the LORD."

— PSALM 112:6-7

I will never forget the day my daughter split her chin open when she fell off of a scooter while playing outside. I don't mean it was just a deep cut that bled a lot. I mean her chin had a giant hole that, I kid you not, resembled the Sarlacc pit from *Return of the Jedi*. If you aren't familiar with that movie, Google it, and you'll understand my sheer panic.

My mind was racing faster than the car as we drove to the hospital. How much pain was she in? What was the extent of the damage? What would it take to fix this? Would she have a scar? On the outside, I remained calm and reassuring for her, but on the inside, I was in full panic mode.

Looking back, I'm embarrassed that I claim to have such a strong faith, yet forgot to trust God in this moment of crisis. I forgot that, even if the news was not good, that I didn't need to dread it because God would help us deal with it.

Why is it so much harder to obey God's command not to worry when our kids are involved?

To combat this temptation to worry, you and I need to build a habit of turning our children over to God in faith and trust before the crisis hits so that in the moment of crisis, trusting God is our default mode, not our last resort. To do this, you can:

- Pray for your child daily.
- Verbally express your faith in God's plan and protection for your children.
- Pray with your children when you feel anxious and sense that they do too.
- Begin with a rote (memorized) prayer when crisis hits.

How do you respond when you're afraid for your child? How could you more actively build your habit of calling on the Lord in faith and trust when concern or crisis hits for your children?

Jesus, in moments of concern and crisis for my children, remind me to trust in You completely. Fill me with Your peace, which surpasses all understanding, and reassure me that I need not worry because, regardless of the outcome, You will carry me and my kids through it all.

PSALM 46:2-3 · PSALM 34:5

74 **unsettled**

"I will restore my people Israel, they shall rebuild and inhabit their ruined cities, plant vineyards and drink the wine, set out gardens and eat the fruits. I will plant them upon their own ground; never again shall they be plucked from the land I have given them—the LORD, your God, has spoken."

— AMOS 9:14-15

The kids and I moved eight times before they even finished elementary school. Each time we got settled somewhere, it was time to pack up and move again. There were a variety of drivers behind the moves—finances, childcare, and the pursuit of an increasingly better living situation as I tried to rebuild after the divorce. One factor remained consistent amidst all of the moves—the feeling of being displaced.

Most of the moves were to places that I knew would be temporary. As we stayed with family or in rentals, we longed to be settled, to truly be home. We spent over a decade feeling like nomads before we were finally able to settle into a house that would truly be our home, and during that period of waiting, I battled uncertainty and doubt that God would ever help us find a place to call our own. It had been so long that it felt like it might never happen.

Unfortunately, many, if not most, single parents struggle with housing instability at some point. Whether you've moved often, faced homelessness, worried about how to hang onto your home in tough times, or had to move out of the place where you thought you would raise your kids, I imagine that you too have encountered that uncomfortable sense of being displaced. You may have also found yourself questioning if God's promises to restore, rebuild, and provide security were really for you.

If you've been there or are experiencing this now, I hope Amos 9:14-15 brings you as much hope and certainty in God's good plan for you as it did for me. On the surface, it reads like many of the promises of Scripture, but the last few words drive home the reality of God's intentions for you to be restored, rebuilt, and settled.

Throughout Scripture, we see that God's spoken word has power. By His words, Heaven and Earth and all living creatures came to be. We see repeatedly throughout the Bible that when God speaks, things happen. Well, guess what, my friend? In Amos 9:14-15, the promise of restoration ends with the words, "the LORD, your God, has spoken."

When He speaks, things happen. Even as you wait to once again feel settled and "at home," you can be sure God is working to bring good into your life. He spoke a promise to bring new life, joy, and goodness from what was once ruined, not just back in history but now in the present for you too. You will eventually feel settled and at home once again, and until then, you can cling tightly to the promise that God spoke over you and your children.

What area of your life feels unsettled or displaced right now? Spend some time today meditating on God's spoken promise in Amos and express your trust in God to restore, rebuild, and settle in your life.

Jesus, please replace my doubt with certainty that I can trust in Your promise to restore, rebuild, and settle us. Pour out Your grace upon me and my children to help us feel "at home" no matter where we are as long as we are together.

PSALM 33:9 · EZEKIEL 12:25

75 rebuilding

"...the LORD, your God, will restore your fortunes and will have compassion on you; he will again gather you from all the peoples where the LORD, your God, has scattered you."

— DEUTERONOMY 30:3

Rebuilding after becoming a single parent can feel like a herculean task. In the split from the other parent, you likely lost a lot, perhaps half of everything, if not more. Letting go of the material things like the dishes that had once been a wedding gift or the furniture that you bought together for your first home is painful.

On top of rebuilding financially, you have to rebuild emotionally, mentally, spiritually, and sometimes, physically too. It's overwhelming to contemplate starting over, but you know that, for the sake of your children, you have no choice but to figure out how to rebuild.

Praise God that you do not have to face this task alone because God's promise of restoration covers all areas of your life. Did you know that when restoration is mentioned in Scripture it is often accompanied by the promise that God will restore double what you lost? Sit with that truth for a minute.

The story of Job is a great example of this from the Old Testament. In Chapter 1 of the Book of Job, we read how Job literally lost everything, and yet, he chose to continue to trust God. In Job 42:10, we read that in the end "...the LORD even gave to Job twice as much as he had before." This promise is for you too.

Right now, it may feel as though you've lost everything, but God is not going to leave you there. If you continue to walk faithfully with Him, He will, in time, change your situation. Every ounce of restoration that we experience is a gift from God, but He is calling us to actively participate in the process.

- **Financial restoration:** pursue a new job opportunity that He puts in front of you even if it's intimidating to think of making the move or seek education and new skills to better position you for a future job opportunity.

- **Mental and emotional restoration:** prayerfully consider seeking support from a professional counselor, even if you're like me and typically prefer to keep things private and work through challenges independently.
- **Spiritual restoration:** if your situation merits it, seek help from the Tribunal Advocate at your parish to petition for an annulment, which is not just bureaucracy and paperwork but is actually a healing process whether you plan to remarry in the future or not.

How is God calling you to partner with Him in bringing restoration to your life?

Jesus, in Your compassion, restore what has been lost in my life. Give me hope for what is to come and show me how I am meant to partner with You to rebuild and bring about this restoration.

JOB 42:10 · JEREMIAH 30:3

76 cleansing habits

"If iniquity is in your hand, remove it, and do not let injustice dwell in your tent, surely then you may lift up your face in innocence; you may stand firm and unafraid."

— JOB 11:14-15

My friend, it's time for a tough topic. Please know that I'm here to offer encouragement and empathy, not judgment. I'm fighting similar battles. We're in this together.

Let's have an honest conversation. Are you clinging to a sin that you need to confront and confess? That's kind of broad, so let's get more specific. Are you clinging to a sin because it brings you pleasure or comfort?

As a single parent, you're overworked, tired, and often lonely. You get little to no affection beyond the hugs from your children, and most nights end with you alone. There's no one with which to share your day or to share a laugh. Under these circumstances, it's easy to convince yourself that you deserve what little pleasure or comfort come your way, even if it doesn't line up with how you know God wants you to live.

You may also be unconsciously trying to numb or shut out your emotions because, deep down, you don't want to face them. Without thinking about it, you gravitate toward things that bring you pleasure or comfort and mindlessly indulge. Some of the ways that people try to find pleasure or numb their emotions include:

- Binging TV or endlessly scrolling social media
- Consuming unhealthy foods
- Drinking alcohol too frequently or in large amounts
- Taking drugs
- Having sex or watching pornography

If one or more of the bullet points on that list resonate with you, there's a good chance you're holding on to a sin that you need to confront and confess. As much as you absolutely do deserve pleasure, comfort, relaxation, and affection, this is not the way that God intended you to find those things. It's difficult to collaborate with God or even hear God when you're clinging to sin.

It can be hard to go to confession when you haven't been in a long time, have held on to a sin for longer than you should have, or feel embarrassed by what you need to confess. But I assure you, Jesus is waiting for you with open arms, and you're not going to say anything the priest hasn't heard before.

There is one caveat: For your confession to be valid, you need to have intention to give up your sin. But don't let that hold you back. Go to confession. You won't regret it. I always feel better when I'm back in right relationship with Jesus and breaking bad habits that are causing more harm than good. You will too.

As you consider your habits, do you feel convicted that you're holding on to a sin for the purpose of seeking comfort or pleasure? To what extent are you ready to confront, confess, and abandon that behavior?

Jesus, I know I have unconfessed sin that is keeping me from right relationship with You and the Church. Show me the habits I need to change, allow me to make a good confession, and give me the resolve to create new, healthy habits.

ISAIAH 59:2 · ROMANS 6:1-4

77 redeemed

"For the grace of God has appeared, saving all and training us to reject godless ways and worldly desires and to live temperately, justly, and devoutly in this age, as we await the blessed hope, the appearance of the glory of the great God and of our savior Jesus Christ, who gave himself for us to deliver us from all lawlessness and to cleanse for himself a people as his own, eager to do what is good."

— TITUS 2:11-14

What if I told you that your life hasn't been ruined but rather redeemed since you became a single parent?

I know that you're facing many difficulties right now because even when things are "good" for a single parent, life is still extra challenging. I also know that, at times, your suffering can make it feel like your life is in ruins and that you're being unfairly punished right now.

In the Old Testament books, such as Genesis and Numbers, we read of suffering endured as a result of disobeying God. In Hebrews 12, in the New Testament, Paul tells us that our trials may be discipline from God. Even though I know Jesus' message is of mercy and love, I've felt, at times, like my suffering and trials might be a punishment. I'm certainly not perfect, but I couldn't figure out why I was suffering more than others for such an extended period. I couldn't figure out why my life seemed to be in ruins when I had tried so hard to follow God.

It took me a long time to realize that the suffering we endure isn't necessarily a punishment. (We've touched on this before, but it's worth repeating!) Rather than being a punishment, suffering can actually be restorative and help us build the habit of relying on God instead of on ourselves and worldly comforts.

If you view your situation through this lens, you'll probably find that, through the suffering you've endured as a single parent, you've grown closer to God and to who He wants you to be. Perhaps, you're even closer to being the person God has called you to be than you ever would have been without these struggles.

I know that is true for me. I'm more compassionate, patient, humble, and self-giving, just to name a few, and I'm closer to God than I ever was at any other point in my life.

The more I thought about the restorative nature of suffering, the more I realized that my life isn't ruined. It's redeemed in ways I didn't even know needed to be redeemed.

Saint Thérèse of Lisieux once said, "I had to pass through many trials before reaching the haven of peace, before tasting the delicious fruits of perfect love and of complete abandonment to God's will."

How has the suffering that you've experienced as a single parent redeemed your character or habits in surprising or notable ways? What happens to your perspective on your suffering when you view these trials as God loving you so perfectly that He wants to help you let go of anything that is not bringing you closer to Him?

Jesus, on the hard days when I look around me and feel like my life is in ruins, allow me to shift my focus from the suffering to all of the ways You are redeeming me through this situation. Remind me that You will use the trials in my life to bring me closer to You if I continue to turn to You in love and trust.

HEBREWS 12:5-7 · PSALM 25:1-2

78 clearing the clutter

"...since he is not the God of disorder but of peace."

— 1 CORINTHIANS 14:33

Some days are so busy that I just can't keep all of the balls in the air anymore. Something has to drop, and the ball that I usually drop first is keeping the house neat and organized. I love having a tidy house with everything in its place, so it doesn't take long for the mess to drive me crazy. Once a little clutter builds, it seems to quickly multiply into hefty and unmanageable piles that drain my energy and frustrate me every time I look at them.

You might be facing the same thing at your house. It could be toys, dirty (or clean) laundry, dishes, or mail. Whatever the pile is, it irritates you when you see it, but it can be hard to muster the energy to tackle it even when you do have the time. If your household is like mine, this clutter can create a lot of discord between you and your kids too. I wouldn't be surprised if you told me that the more aggravated you are with your own mess, the more likely you are to snap at the kids about their mess. I know that's how it works at my house!

When I finally hit my limit with the mess, I find that tackling just one pile makes me feel so much better that it often builds momentum to knock out a few more piles of clutter. Have you ever noticed how good you feel after clearing the clutter? There is a peace that comes from restoring order in your home, and if you look at 1 Corinthians 14:33, you'll understand why.

This passage tells us that God is not the God of disorder. You might expect that to be followed up with the explanation that He is the God of order, but instead it says He is the God of peace. Why does it say "peace" instead of "order"? I would propose it's because the clutter and mess steal our peace.

When God inspires you to declutter, you might also sense that He's calling you to simplify by letting go of things you no longer need. In the Gospel of Matthew, Jesus tells the rich young man to sell what he has and come follow Him. The message here isn't just about letting go of the desire for possessions. It's also about simplifying your life so you can be at peace and have more freedom to follow Jesus.

We often have clutter in our souls, minds, or hearts too, such as sin or regret, that can also distract us from being able to hear Jesus. How often does this kind of clutter rob us of peace too?

What pile in your house, body, mind, heart, or soul is God urging you to tackle today?

Start small with a task that you can complete in ten minutes or less. Don't think about it or give into the temptation to keep putting it off. Just take the first step to start clearing the clutter, and along the way, toss or donate anything that you don't need anymore. Before you even finish, a sense of relief will start to wash over you, and when that annoying pile is finally gone, you might just find that the satisfaction and peace are enough to motivate you to keep the clutter-clearing momentum going!

Jesus, help me find the time and energy to clear out any clutter that has accumulated in my life, so I can bring peace to my children and to my home. Show me how to simplify my surroundings so I can be free to focus on You.

MATTHEW 19:21 · PROVERBS 15:16

79 **waiting well**

"Wait for the LORD, take courage;
be stouthearted, wait for the LORD!"

— PSALM 27:14

Most single parents I know have a deep longing for companionship. Even if you've been hurt or find it hard to trust, you likely ache for companionship.

In Genesis, God explicitly says, "It is not good for man to be alone." You were made for relationship, which is why it is so hard to understand when God does not swiftly answer your prayer for companionship.

During the waiting, you may be tempted to:

- Date someone you know is probably not who God would choose for you.
- Settle for someone who meets a need, such as providing financial security, but with whom you do not have true emotional intimacy.
- Choose someone who leads you away from God and toward sin.
- Fall for someone who will take advantage of your vulnerability.

- Skip dating and marriage and jump right to a physical relationship for temporary comfort.

No doubt, loneliness can lead us to bad choices and a lot of regret. I know from my own experience that the longer the loneliness goes on, the easier it is to talk yourself into believing you have a valid excuse for making one of these questionable choices.

When you find yourself tempted to make bad choices driven by loneliness or just simply find yourself tired of being alone, try taking one (or all) of the steps below:

- Renew your trust in God, even if the waiting has been long.
- Do something good for God in service to others with like-minded people, which will increase your chances of meeting the one God has for you.
- Remember that you can fill your companionship bucket through non-romantic relationships too.
- Wait with stouthearted resolve to pursue only companionship that brings you closer to God, fills you with peace and joy, and helps you become a better-version-of-yourself.

That last one is a biggie.

How are you coping with your longing for companionship? Which step could you try today to ease the ache in a productive, God-centered way?

Jesus, I know You are aware of my loneliness. Please show me how to delight in You as I wait for You to fulfill my desire for companionship according to Your will.

PSALM 37:3-4 · PSALM 31:25

80 silence the noise

"For thus said the Lord GOD, the Holy One of Israel: By waiting and by calm you shall be saved, in quiet and in trust shall be your strength."

— ISAIAH 30:15

We live in a noisy world. As I climb into bed at night, I hear crowds cheering and scores being announced from the neighbor's TV that is mounted outside on his back patio. Anywhere out in public, there is inevitably someone playing music or videos out loud on their phone with no regard for who it disturbs. Even at church, I can hear traffic and sirens outside.

At home, you and I contribute to this problem by filling our lives with more noise. Of course, the kids are naturally noisy, but if you're like me, you add to the noise by constantly playing music, running the TV in the background of other activities, and filling the quiet moments in your day by scrolling through social media.

It's almost impossible to find silence anywhere anymore. Is it any wonder that we find it hard to hear God?

In Scripture, God repeatedly tells us how to hear Him, and it generally comes down to two actions that we need to take: be still and be quiet. These two actions usually go hand-in-hand.

In the Biblical sense, to "be still" means more than stopping movement. It's a call to cease striving and struggling and an invitation to let God have control.

Once you are still, you're ready to listen, but you can't hear God if you perpetually drown out the silence with noise. To hear God's still, small voice, you also need quiet.

I love music just as much, if not more, than the next person. Being the only adult in my house, I also enjoy a witty, well-written show or movie to make me laugh as I knock out chores or close out my evening alone. There's a time and place for both, but I've noticed that I sometimes keep the noise going to distract myself because I know that, when I turn the noise off, my mind will start churning over thoughts or feelings I'd rather ignore. Maybe you do the same.

If you take an honest look at your home environment, how are you adding to the noise in your life and distracting yourself from thinking deeply and clearly? What would your life look like if you spent just five or ten minutes in true silence every day?

Jesus, I am tempted to fill my life with endless noise and distraction when I actually need to be still and quiet. Help me to choose quiet so I can hear You when You speak.

PSALM 46:11 · 1 KINGS 19:11-12

81 **the anniversary**

"...Do not be saddened this day, for rejoicing in the LORD is your strength!"

— NEHEMIAH 8:10

Eventually, "that day" arrives. The day when all of the memories come flooding back. The day when you wonder if one different decision along the way would have allowed it all to turn out differently. The day when your heart breaks a little and you just can't hold back the tears, even though you thought you were over it. Yes, it's the anniversary.

Maybe it's the wedding anniversary or the anniversary of the event that led to you becoming a single parent. Whatever it is and however much you've healed, there's a wave of sadness that washes over you on this day. I know because the same thing happens to me.

It's tempting to unravel on these days as you battle the regret, grief, guilt, anger, and disappointment with how it all turned out. That's exactly where Satan wants you to stay because he knows that if he can keep you looking backward, you won't be looking forward to all of the good things God has planned for you.

The trick to surviving these days is to immerse yourself in reminders of God's love for you. One way that I do this is by looking at photos of special moments I've shared with the kids and reflecting on the gift of having children. I see God's love in their smiles.

Rejoicing in the Lord is truly your strength, but that does not mean that you shouldn't ever cry. If you're blinking back the tears, let them fall down your cheeks and have a good, cathartic cry. But then, turn your face to God and accept His invitation out of the darkness and into the light.

When you see "that day" approaching on the calendar, plan for how you will fill the day with things that bring you joy and help you make positive progress toward a future goal.

- Get off of the couch and go for a walk in the sunshine.
- Create new memories with your kids.
- Watch a movie or a show that makes you belly laugh (a genuine smile triggers endorphins, which signal to your body that you're happy and, in turn, make you actually feel happier).
- Learn something new.
- Tackle that bookshelf or closet that you want to organize.

Even a small amount of progress will feel satisfying and will give you the sense of forward momentum away from what was and toward all that God has for you.

How could you immerse yourself in God's love the next time "that day" rolls around, or maybe even today? What bit of positive progress could you make that would lift your spirit from darkness to light?

Jesus, release me from the memories about what "that day" once was and from any lingering sadness I may have about "that day." Show me how to fill my day with Your peace and joy so I will have the strength to face my feelings and let them go.

PSALM 30:6 · LUKE 1:78-79

82 being present

"As they continued their journey, he entered a village where a woman whose name was Martha welcomed him. She had a sister named Mary [who] sat beside the Lord at his feet listening to him speak. Martha, burdened with much serving, came to him and said, 'Lord, do you not care that my sister has left me by myself to do the serving? Tell her to help me.' The Lord said to her in reply, 'Martha, Martha, you are anxious and worried about many things. There is need of only one thing. Mary has chosen the better part and it will not be taken from her.'"

— LUKE 10:38-42

How many times have you been so busy trying to make the birthday party or holiday perfect for your child that you missed out on actually being present to soak up your child's joy and excitement during the event? This happens to me more often than I'd like to admit.

As the sole parent, you feel like it's on you to make all the preparations, take all the pictures, serve all the treats, refill all the drinks, facilitate the activities, and clean up the mess. It's enough to make you empathize with Martha who was working to be the perfect hostess and feeling a bit resentful that her sister Mary did nothing to help during Jesus' visit to their home.

Jesus noticed and appreciated all that Martha did for Him during His visit, but what He'd have enjoyed even more would have been for Martha to stop and sit with Him as Mary did. The same is true of our kids. Your child delights in having your focused attention. Your child will remember laughing with you and playing with you during a celebration long after his or her memory of the food or gift fades, and your weary spirit will be renewed from this special time together.

The same is true of Jesus. He delights in having your focused attention, and He longs to connect with you and renew your weary spirit. Pausing to be fully present with Him will calm your soul and better equip you for what lies ahead. It's not indulgent to take a moment and sit with Jesus. It is exactly what you need.

Being fully present with Jesus gives you the grace to be fully present with your children.

In what ways could you be more fully present with Jesus? In what ways would you like to be more fully present with your kids?

Jesus, help me to pause and be fully present with You. Please give me the grace and awareness to be fully present with my kids too, particularly when I am tired and feel pressed to focus on the chores or work instead of on them.

ISAIAH 55:6 · JOB 33:33

83 trusting God's plan

"For my thoughts are not your thoughts, nor are your ways my ways—oracle of the LORD. For as the heavens are higher than the earth, so are my ways higher than your ways, my thoughts higher than your thoughts."

— ISAIAH 55:8-9

Have you ever gone skydiving? I have, and I can tell you it's all fun and games until the plane door opens.

On the day I jumped, I was chatting with the instructor on the plane as we climbed to the needed altitude. In the video of my skydiving jump, you can see that when the door opened, I got very still, and my expression changed from jovial to contemplative. In that moment, I remember thinking, "That's not right. That door should NOT be open."

As I stepped up to the edge of the doorway and prepared to jump, everything in me was screaming, "What are you doing? Get back in the plane!" And then, suddenly, I was tumbling out of the plane headfirst, placing complete trust in my instructor (who was strapped to my back) to bring us safely to the ground. It was one of the most beautiful, weirdly peaceful, yet exhilarating, and rewarding experiences of my life, and I would have missed it if I hadn't trusted my instructor enough to take the leap.

Trusting God's plan when it's not what you want or doesn't make sense is a lot like skydiving.

God opens a door unexpectedly. It may even be a door you had no desire to walk through, but it's clear that He wants you move. At first, you're disoriented, and things don't look right. All you can think is, "Uh God, are You sure? I don't think it's supposed to be this way."

Then, God brings you to the doorway, and He asks you to step out in faith and try something big. He promises to equip you and protect you, but for this to work, you have to trust Him completely. It looks like it could be an amazing opportunity, but you're just not sure where it's going to lead.

You have a choice to make. Are you going to jump or stay on the plane?

In what area of your life is God asking you to step out in faith and trust His plan, even though you're not sure where it will lead? Are you ready to jump? If not, why?

Jesus, You have placed an opportunity in front of me and seem to be asking me to step out in faith to pursue it. Give me wisdom to discern Your will and help me to trust Your plan for my life, especially if You're taking me somewhere I never expected to go.

PHILIPPIANS 1:6 · ROMANS 8:28

84 **rising to the occasion**

"For God is at work in you, both to will and to work for his good pleasure."

— PHILIPPIANS 2:13

There is a good chance that the day that you buckled your newborn into the car and drove away from the hospital for the first time was the day that the magnitude of what it meant to be a parent set in. On that ride home, the thought of being responsible for another human being for the next eighteen years probably felt like a daunting task, and rightfully so. You may have even questioned if you were ready for the challenge. If you didn't question it that day, you certainly questioned it on the day you became a single parent and wondered, "How will I do this alone?"

And yet, here you are rising to the occasion.

No matter how old your children are or how long you've been a single parent, you need to pause and give yourself a giant pat on the back for the love and dedication you've poured into fulfilling your responsibilities as a parent. If you don't, you risk losing sight of the fact that what you're doing is *extraordinary,* not ordinary, and you risk dwelling on your less-than-perfect moments instead of how you carry this responsibility with grace and strength most of the time. You should feel so proud of what you've accomplished so far.

The good news is that, even as a single parent, you are not raising your children alone. God is by your side and leading the way. He is your parenting partner, and He will bless you and your children in special ways because He knows the extra challenges that you face. Your difficulties have been two-fold, so He wants your joy to be two-fold too.

As you celebrate your parenting achievements, I encourage you to give thanks to God for guiding you and providing for you along the way. In doing so, you avoid the traps of pride outlined in Scripture because you are giving credit to God. It's good, even healthy, to feel proud of yourself and how hard you have worked when you give glory to God for making all this possible. After all, He is the one who works in you to desire and to work for His good purpose, but you are the one who is responding to His call and doing the hard work of parenting. You are a perfect team.

Parenting is one of the most difficult, but rewarding, things that you'll do in your life. So today, take a deep breath, smile, and reflect on all that you've overcome and sacrificed to make it this far in your parenting journey. You've stepped up and done well.

Through God's grace, you will find the strength and perseverance to continue this journey. I pray that you pause often along the way to take pride in your efforts as you watch your children learn and grow because of how you've stepped up to fulfill your responsibilities as a parent. And remember that you're never doing this alone.

Jesus, please remind me that it is okay to take great pride in the love and dedication that I pour into parenting as long as I also give You glory for partnering with me on this parenting journey. Help me to continue rising to the occasion in my solo parenting mission.

ROMANS 15:17-18 · ISAIAH 61:7

85 clarity

"Therefore, do not make any judgment before the appointed time, until the Lord comes, for he will bring to light what is hidden in darkness and will manifest the motives of our hearts, and then everyone will receive praise from God."

— 1 CORINTHIANS 4:5

Have you ever felt so sure you were pursuing God's will only to find out later it was not the right path? If so, you know it's hard to make sense of the heartache, confusion, and disappointment of realizing you pursued the wrong goal, especially when you thought you were following God's will. And you know how difficult it is to figure out what's next as you second guess yourself and think, "How could it have been so wrong if it felt like I was on the right path? How can I trust myself to choose more wisely next time?"

When I was a freshman in high school, I loved football and was convinced that my calling was to work in marketing for a professional football team. I ended up going to college on a "football scholarship" where I worked in equipment, recruiting, game day operations, and marketing, and I was eventually hired for a marketing internship with the Dallas Cowboys. Standing on the field at Texas Stadium for the first time as part of the team felt like a dream come true, and I was convinced that I was where God meant for me to be.

I loved my time with the Cowboys, but it didn't take long for me to sense that, in my excitement to pursue this passion, I had overlooked aspects of this career that did not seem to align with my values, including how my weekends would be full of work instead of church. As I pondered my situation,

I realized that I had mistaken passion for clear leading from God. The only thing I could do was take a step back and ask God, "What's next?" And this time, I listened before leaping into a new career.

With God, all things ARE possible, but that doesn't mean that all things are His will for you. You can save yourself time and effort AND feel confident about your choices when you ask yourself these two questions:

1. Am I pursuing this for the right reasons and for an outcome that would be pleasing to God?
2. Am I doing this for God's glory or my own?

These questions remove emotion from the situation long enough to take an objective look at the reasons why you want to pursue an opportunity. In my situation, pursuing football was for my glory, not His. It's not that football itself is bad. There are many athletes who use sports as a platform to evangelize. But my underlying motivation for choosing the career was not grounded in a desire to please God or give God glory. If I had asked myself these questions, I probably would have chosen a different path altogether.

How is God inviting you to apply these questions to an upcoming opportunity in your life or in your kids' lives?

Jesus, guide me as I determine which opportunities my children and I should pursue. Give me the wisdom to know if a feeling of excitement means that I am on the right track or that I should slow down and consider if the outcome will lead me closer to You.

PROVERBS 14:12 · PHILIPPIANS 1:9-10

86 **unanswered prayers**

"And we have this confidence in him, that if we ask anything according to his will, he hears us."

—1 JOHN 5:14

There are many Scriptures that seem to indicate that all we have to do is ask, and God will give us what we've requested. Taken out of context, these passages can make God sound more like a genie in a lamp granting wishes than a loving Father.

Even still, when your faith is strong, you want to approach God with confidence as you make your requests, knowing that He can move mountains if you have faith the size of a mustard seed. When He doesn't answer or seems to answer differently than you had hoped, it's tempting to wonder, "Was my faith not big enough?" It can be hard to make sense of why God would not want you or your child to have this seemingly good thing.

Personally, I've struggled with this as I've prayed for over a decade to find the spouse that God has for me, but I am still alone. I've scoured the Scriptures looking for answers, and I finally realized what the problem, or rather *problems* plural, might be:

- For some reason, what I was requesting, however good it may have been, was not God's will for me.
- My request stemmed from a desire to follow my passions instead of seeking and following God's will for my life.

This realization left me with a lot of questions. Why wouldn't God want me to be loved and married? Why was it bad to want to share my life with someone? Was I just supposed to be alone forever? I thought we were made for relationships. In Genesis, didn't God say it was bad for man to be alone?

It took me awhile to find the *right* questions to ask, but I finally got there:

- If this is not God's will for me, will that be the case forever. . . or just for now?
- What is God's will for my life right now?
- Is my faith strong enough to accept God's will, even if it's different than what I want for myself?
- What should I be seeking right now in place of this passion?

If you're struggling to make sense of your own unanswered prayer, I'd encourage you to ask yourself these same questions. And to offer some reassurance, I'll let you in on a secret. If I had gotten remarried when I wanted to, I never would have written this book. It's taken over a decade, but God finally revealed to me why His will was different than what I would have chosen for myself. And I still have hope that this is a "for now" and not a "forever" situation.

Is your faith strong enough to follow God's will for your life? You never know where He might be leading you!

Jesus, give me an unwavering faith in Your will for my life, even when it's different than what I deeply desire, and help me to seek Your will amidst my "unanswered" prayers.

JOHN 16:24 · JAMES 4:3

87 **pray without ceasing**

"Rejoice always. Pray without ceasing."

— 1 THESSALONIANS 5:16-17

During the holiday season, life seems to ratchet up to an even more frantic pace than usual with all the kids' activities and preparations for Christmas. In my tired and busy state, my "quiet time" is shorter than usual, or worse, it's filled with distractions.

Do you ever find yourself struggling to make prayer a priority during the holidays? Maybe you sit down with good intentions to pray, but somehow, you end up on your phone ordering a last-minute gift instead of talking to God. Or maybe you arrive home so late from the school Christmas concert that you forget to say bedtime prayers with the kids. I have found myself facing the same challenges.

One day in confession, I mentioned my failure to pray and explained that I could not find any quiet time in my day to focus on prayer. The very kind priest in the confessional reminded me that God doesn't care where we pray. While it is impactful to pray in a quiet place, you can also weave prayer into the busyness of your day. This seems like common sense, and yet, it took intentionality on my part to make this a habit.

Saint Elizabeth Ann Seton once said, "We must pray without ceasing, in every occurrence and employment of our lives—that prayer which is rather a habit of lifting up the heart to God as in a constant communication with Him." She echoes the words that I heard from the priest. God doesn't care where you pray. He just wants to hear from you. The more constant your communication with Him, the better.

You can talk to Him while you wash dishes. You can pray in the carpool line instead of scrolling through social media while you wait. You can praise Him while you shower. You can drive or ride to work in silence instead of listening to news and podcasts. You can say bedtime prayers with the kids in the car on the way home from the concert at school. God is delighted when you draw Him deeper into your life by praying throughout the day.

Whether you have plenty of time to pray in silence or you're squeezing in a Hail Mary during soccer practice, God is overjoyed and ready to listen.

How could you weave more prayer into the busyness of your day today?

Jesus, direct my thoughts toward You throughout my day and remind me to persevere in prayer no matter where I am or what I am doing. Thank You for hearing my prayers even when I cannot be fully still and present with You while I pray.

ROMANS 12:12 · LUKE 18:1

88 **wise decisions**

"In the morning let me hear of your mercy, for in you I trust. Show me the path I should walk, for I entrust my life to you."

— PSALM 143:8

During the early days of being a single parent, I sometimes felt paralyzed when facing big decisions that I had to make without the comfort and support of a spouse. Sound familiar?

That feeling of being stuck when facing a big decision is not a one-time sensation. It sneaks up on you at random times throughout the parenting journey as Satan subtly says, "Remember when you made that terrible choice, and it wrecked your life? You might make the wrong choice now too." You suddenly feel unsure of what to do next as you strain to discern the best path while silently questioning whether or not you can trust yourself to make the right decision.

The good news is that you don't have to make big decisions alone. Jesus is always there waiting for you to invite Him into the process. He may directly help you decide. But don't be surprised if Jesus also shines a light on whom you should consult as you make this decision. He often speaks to us through the people that He puts in our lives.

What big decision lies before you at the moment? Have you brought your situation and uncertainty before the Lord and prayed for clarity to follow His will? If not, why? If so, where is He leading you?

Always remember that you are more than a poor decision that you may have made in the past. You are well equipped to make decisions for yourself and for your children when you invite Jesus into the process and seek wisdom to inform your decision.

Jesus, please give me wisdom to discern Your will for this situation and to choose the path that will be best for me and my children. Help me to seek out and recognize people that you have placed in my life to help me make wise decisions.

JEREMIAH 17:7 · JAMES 1:5

89 **guardian angels**

"For he commands his angels with regard to you, to guard you wherever you go. With their hands they shall support you, lest you strike your foot against a stone."

— PSALM 91:11-12

Within five minutes of turning on the news, you will inevitably hear a tragic story involving a child. As a parent it is so hard to hear these stories, especially the stories of senseless violence involving kids, like school shootings, drunk driving accidents, and child abductions.

A friend of mine is a news anchor and a mother. She is immersed in these heartbreaking stories every day at work, and she can't help but feel the fear for her own children bubble up as she contemplates the randomness of these tragedies. You don't have to work in the news industry or even watch the news daily to experience fear for your kids' safety as you send them out into the world.

The Scriptures are filled with the words, "Do not be afraid." God does not want you to live in fear, even in this unpredictable world. One of my favorite ways to live free from fear is to call on God's angels for help and protection, especially the kids' guardian angels.

Saint Jerome, an early Church father, once said: "How great the dignity of the soul, since each one has from his birth an angel commissioned to guard it." Angels are real, and God commands them to guard you and your children.

God told us there would be trouble in this world, and sometimes, tragedies do still occur. But you can take an active role in protecting your kids by asking God to send His angels with your kids wherever they go.

One way to do this is to say a Prayer to Your Guardian Angel with your kids:

> *Angel of God, my guardian dear, to whom God's love commits me here,*
> *ever this day be at my side, to light and guard, to rule and guide.*
> *Amen.*

Another way is to say my mom's prayer. Anytime my kids and I leave my parents' house, my mom says, "Angels go with you." There is a very real peace that comes from this simple prayer.

However you choose to fight the fear, invite your guardian angel and your children's guardian angels into the process. There is peace in knowing your children have a special protector with them at all times.

What level of fear do you hold about sending your kids out into the world, particularly as they get older and go more places without you? Is there a way that you could more actively and proactively pray for protection over your family?

Jesus, it's tempting to feel afraid as I send my children out into this crazy, unpredictable world. Cover my family in Your protection, send Your angels to guard us wherever we go, and give us peace.

PSALM 34:8 · DANIEL 6:23

90 savor the moments

"When a woman is in labor, she is in anguish because her hour has arrived; but when she has given birth to a child, she no longer remembers the pain because of her joy that a child has been born into the world."

— JOHN 16:21

A country singer named Trace Adkins released a song called "You're Gonna Miss This" right around the time I became a new single parent with a newborn and a one-year-old. I was overwhelmed and exhausted as I coped with grieving the loss of my marriage and parenting such young children alone. I wasn't sure how I would make it through the next eighteen years, but this song reminded me—as hard as this was—that there would be a day when I would miss those little babies and the precious moments from this season of life.

At the time, it was hard to believe I would miss being awake almost around the clock and changing endless diapers, but I've found the words from that song to be true over and over. In time, whatever difficulties you're experiencing in your current season of parenting will be overshadowed by the cherished memories from that same period of time. You will indeed miss "this" somewhere down the road.

Sometimes, we're so busy trying to get through the hard thing that we forget to savor the good along the way. God doesn't want you to miss these precious moments with your kids only to look back one day and wish you had been more present with them and more grateful for the good times at each stage of their childhood.

One parenting responsibility I thought I would NEVER miss were the hours spent driving the kids to and from school and activities. I was beyond excited for my son to get his driver's license so he could make all the trips himself and give his sister rides too. But the day he got his license, I was shocked to discover that I was actually going to miss this time in the car with both my kids.

A sadness washed over me as it occurred to me that, in my longing for a break from the frequent trips, I had taken our time in the car for granted. The car was a place where we had one-on-one time, some of our most meaningful conversations, rowdy sing-alongs, and so many laughs. Now, seemingly so suddenly (even though it was sixteen years in the making), that chapter came to a close.

No matter how old your children are, I bet you too can look back and find moments that once felt like a chore but were actually special times with your kids. When you think of caring for your newborn, the memory of the extreme fatigue likely fades as you wish you could go back and rock that little baby once again. When you look back at when your kids were toddlers, the weariness of being needed constantly fades as you wish you could go back to when your small child would climb in your lap and ask to read stories with you.

In John 16:21, God explains that the hardships of parenting will pass and are quickly overshadowed by the joy your children bring to you. It's challenging to remember that in the moment, but if you keep this truth in the forefront of your mind, it will change how you experience parenting, especially on the hard days.

What parenting hardship are you facing today? What are the "good times" amidst this hardship that God is inviting you to savor today before you "miss this" at some point in time down the road?

Jesus, help me to notice and appreciate the good times with my children that I may overlook amidst the busyness of our days. One day, as I look back and miss this, give me peace that I made the most of these precious moments with my kids.

PSALM 127:3-4 · ECCLESIASTES 3:1

91 **accepting help**

"Whoever confers benefits will be amply enriched, and whoever refreshes others will be refreshed."

— PROVERBS 11:25

I am the worst about asking for help. I might desperately need help, but pride gets the best of me. I want to prove to myself and others I can do this alone, and I don't want others to see my mess.

Do you find it hard to ask for help sometimes? Whatever your reasons for trying to go it alone, the reality is that you aren't meant to do this alone. Jesus wants you to call on His grace and mercy for help in carrying this load. Inviting Jesus in and asking for His help is usually the easy part. The harder part is asking other people for help.

Think about how it makes you feel when you help others. Helping others feeds your soul and gives you a sense of fulfillment. The same is true for others when you ask them for help.

As I've become open to help in my own life, I've found that God has placed a network of people in my life who are happy to help.

- My dad enjoys providing "Pop's Elite Limo Service" when the kids need rides.
- My mom periodically makes meals to ease the burden of weekly meal prep.
- My sister and her husband provided us with a home and extra support as I transitioned from full-time mom back to the workforce.
- Other parents have cheered my kids on and taken pictures when I couldn't be at events due to work.
- Wonderful neighbors have helped us with home maintenance projects.
- When I was injured, amazing family and friends swarmed to care for the kids and keep the household running while I was out of commission.

Is it humbling to ask for help? Yes, it can be. But it becomes easier when you remember that asking for help is also an opportunity to give others a chance to feed their souls and fulfill God's call for them to serve others.

Who has God placed in your life that could provide much-needed help? Where is He asking you to set pride aside, reach out for help, and enable someone to feel the fulfillment that will come from helping you?

Jesus, please help me to recognize when I need help and give me the humility to ask for it. Allow me to graciously receive the assistance offered by others that You have placed in my life to help meet our needs.

1 THESSALONIANS 5:11 · HEBREWS 13:16

92 sowing bountifully

"Consider this: whoever sows sparingly will also reap sparingly, and whoever sows bountifully will also reap bountifully."

— 2 CORINTHIANS 9:6

Do you ever think to yourself: Life used to be so much simpler? Life certainly used to be simpler for me when my kids were little, and I could, for the most part, control the content they consumed and the people allowed into their circles. Now that they are older and spending more time out in the world on their own, my influence in these areas has decreased, and at times, I've worried about the choices that the kids might make. They are good kids, but even good kids can make bad choices sometimes. I imagine you have the same concerns for your children, even if you actively monitor their online and social activities like I do.

As I struggled with my growing loss of control over the last few years, I came across this powerful quote in a book called *Difficult Teachings* by Matthew Kelly:

> *A lot of worry and anxiety is born because we think we are responsible for things we are not responsible for. So, next time you are anxious and*

worried, ask yourself, "Am I responsible for the thing I am anxious or worried about?" It may be someone else is responsible, and it may be that the things you are worried about is in God's hands and His responsibility.

Wow! Yep, that was me! Realizing that some things are not my responsibility provided great relief and changed my perspective. Now when I start to worry, I know there's a good chance that I'm longing to control something that is God's responsibility, not mine. Then, I do what I can and leave the rest to God. You'll save yourself from a mountain of worry if you adopt the same approach.

You simply can't control all the choices that your kids will make, including whether or not they choose to pursue a relationship with Jesus. All you can do is plant the seeds of faith, wisdom, love, and obedience to God, and then, turn it over to God and let Him do the rest. As it says in 2 Corinthians 9:6, it is your responsibility to "sow bountifully," and if you do, you and your children will reap bountifully too.

"Sowing seeds" means to scatter the seeds where they have a chance to grow. You can't control how the seed grows or the type of fruit it produces. That's in God's hands. You can certainly do what you can along the way to nurture the seed that you planted, but what the seed actually produces is up to how the seed responds to its environment and to God.

So, breathe easier, my friend. You can't control everything, and that's okay because it's not your job to do so. It's God's job, and you can trust Him completely. Just sow the seeds and then watch what God will do.

In what way might you currently be grasping to control something that belongs to God? How could you shift that ownership and responsibility from you back to God?

Jesus, teach me to let go of what is not mine to hold and to focus on my responsibility, which is to sow the seeds that lead my children to open their hearts and minds to God.

1 PETER 5:6-7 · PROVERBS 3:5-6

93 **money matters**

"Let your life be free from love of money but be content with what you have, for he has said, 'I will never forsake you or abandon you.'"

— HEBREWS 13:5

Nothing makes you realize you have an attachment to money like becoming a single parent. Whether you came from a two-income situation or from a one-income situation, expenses tend to go up once you're a single parent. You're maintaining a household alone, generally have greater childcare expenses, and might even be paying more than your share of the kids' expenses.

God tells us to be free from the love of money, but it's hard not to be distracted by finances when you're worried about providing for your kids. You know God wants you to be content with what you have, but it's hard not to look around at two-income families or even at the other parent, who may not have the same financial strain that you do, without feeling discontent, or even jealous.

When these feelings flare up, I find myself asking God, "Why won't you take away the financial strain? Why are you easing the strain for others but not for me?" There's no simple answer to these questions, but there are a few things that you can do to improve your outlook on the financial situation, even if your options for changing the situation are limited right now.

In addition to praying for wisdom in managing your finances, you can:

- Make a budget and stick to it, so you don't multiply the strain by adding debt.
- Put a little money aside each month to save in advance for bigger expenses rather than charging those expenses to credit cards with high interest rates.
- Reflect with gratitude on how God is meeting your financial needs in big and small ways to sustain you and your children day-by-day, such as finding out your car needs a less expensive repair than expected or receiving a small, unexpected influx of money just when you needed it.

You may not be able to fully eliminate the financial strain or longing for more money by budgeting, saving, and focusing on gratitude for what you do have, but prayerfully applying these activities will help you find a greater degree of peace and contentment with your finances.

How is God calling you to adjust your outlook about your finances or your money management habits today?

Jesus, I'm consumed with worry over money, not because I love money itself, but because I want to provide for my children. Give me wisdom in managing our finances, contentment with all that You have already given us, and openness to new opportunities that You may put in my path for improving our financial situation.

1 TIMOTHY 6:7-9 · DEUTERONOMY 8:18

94 **minding the gap**

"While you worked awesome deeds we could not hope for, such as had not been heard of from of old. No ear has ever heard, no eye ever seen, any God but you working such deeds for those who wait for him."

— ISAIAH 64:2-3

I'm normally a big fan of the "something is better than nothing" concept. If I can only spend thirty minutes at the gym instead of an hour, I celebrate that I went to the gym at all and know that thirty minutes of exercise is better than nothing. But that approach rarely yields good results when it comes to choosing who to date.

It can be tempting for single parents to rush into another romantic relationship. The reasons for this vary, but under the surface, there's one primary driver: to fill a gap. That gap could be emotional, physical, financial, social, familial, or functional. Whatever the gap is, the desire to fill it can seem urgent, but choosing a dating partner is definitely something that you don't want to rush.

A few years after my divorce and annulment, I dated a man who initially seemed like he might be the one. He was a strong Catholic, a good dad to his own children, the owner of a successful business, and very much in love with me, but for some reason, I couldn't shake the sense that he was not the one God had chosen for me.

It was tempting to stay with him, as he would have filled many gaps for the kids and me. I think we would have done the same for him, but deep down, I knew that staying with him wasn't the right thing for either of us. It was hard to admit it, but we both knew we would have been settling. The next woman he dated after me eventually became his wife, and they are perfect together. It's clear that she was part of God's plan for him, so I'm thankful I listened to the Holy Spirit and walked away when I did.

He and I both deserved more in a romantic relationship and marriage than just "filling a gap," and so do you.

You might not see it now as you linger in your loneliness, but God has big plans for you and is working to bring good into your life beyond what you can dare hope for or imagine. That might mean falling in love and getting married one day, or it might mean pursuing a different path that is equally beautiful and important but not yet known to you. Even if you're not sure what that plan is yet, you can be certain that who you have by your side as you embark on this new chapter—family, friends, and dating partners alike—will be important. And because your decisions about who to date now affect your kids too, there's more motivation than ever not to settle for less than God's best for you.

If you feel a desire to date or are dating now, are you solely trying to fill gaps in your life and end the loneliness, or are you patiently seeking the partner God has for you?

If you're sensing a gap in your life, how else might you fill it in healthy ways while you wait for God to reveal His plan for you?

Jesus, fill me with peace as I wait in faithful hope and trust for You to show me the plans and partner You have for me. Guide my dating decisions and protect me from settling for less than Your best for my children and me.

PSALM 37:5 · ISAIAH 40:31

95 wandering the wilderness

"A voice proclaims: In the wilderness prepare the way of the LORD! Make straight in the wasteland a highway for our God!"

— ISAIAH 40:3

The dictionary defines the word "wilderness" as a place that is uninhabited and inhospitable. In other words, the wilderness is lonely and provides no shelter or sustenance. Psalm 63 describes the wilderness as parched and lifeless too. Is it any wonder that our experience as single parents can leave us feeling a bit like we're wandering in the wilderness?

One of the most beautiful, and often overlooked, opportunities that God gives us in the wilderness is the chance to prepare for what we've prayed for. My children were very young when I became a single parent, so my most pressing need and prayer was to find a job that would allow me to provide for my family while also being present for my kids as much as possible. God's response to this prayer was to tell me that I should become certified to teach high school.

My career field at the time had nothing to do with teaching, but I followed God's lead and signed up for a certification program. About six months later, I was hired at the high school that was five minutes from where I lived and next door to my children's preschool. Because I responded to His call while I was in the wilderness, I was prepared when He so perfectly answered my prayer.

Without a doubt, you're walking in the wilderness in some aspect of your life right now. Maybe, you are trying to figure out where to live or how to provide for your children's basic needs. Maybe, you're feeling parched as you thirst for life to be about more than just surviving. Whatever your wilderness is, know that God can use it for your good.

In the wilderness, God might test you and allow you to go without in order to teach you to rely on Him. (This has been a difficult lesson for me but one that has left me with deep trust in God and steady joy regardless of my circumstances.) God will also provide for you, strengthen you, and speak to you in ways that are only possible *because* you're in the wilderness.

You have a choice each day. You can wallow in your wilderness, or you can prepare for what you've prayed for. Some days, it's easier than others to step up to this challenge, especially when you've been in the wilderness for a long time. It's normal and, in small doses, healthy to allow yourself to process the feelings of sadness or despair that you might experience in the wilderness. But then you have to decide what's next.

Do you want to remain miserable in your wilderness, or are you ready to prepare for the future that God has planned for you?

How is God inviting you to start preparing for what you've prayed for? What one step could you take today?

Jesus, help me to see past what is difficult, scary, or uncomfortable right now to focus on the good that You have planned for me. Show me how to prepare for what I've prayed for and help me be ready when You reveal what's next for my children and me.

PSALM 63:2 · 2 CHRONICLES 31:21

---

96 **making memories**

"The LORD said to Abram: Go forth from your land, your relatives, and from your father's house to a land that I will show you."

— GENESIS 12:1

Traveling with kids is daunting, especially for single parents. The preparation alone is a monstrous task, and that's followed by more heavy lifting on the trip to manage transportation, luggage, lodging, meals, entertainment, safety, and any surprises that pop up along the way. Oh, and let's not forget the unpacking and laundry once you're back.

The thought of doing all of this alone, especially when the kids are younger and can't help as much, is enough to make you believe it would be easier (and less expensive) to just stay home. But I assure you, it will always be worth it to take the trip. Always.

Whether you travel close to home or somewhere exotic, escaping the grind and exploring somewhere new is good for your kids and you. It's a tremendous amount of work, but God will give you the strength to push through the tough parts and onto the enjoyable aspects of the trip. That doesn't mean the trips will be easy.

Once, after a fun week at the beach, the kids and I spent an hour cramming all our bags and gear into the car. As we set out on our ten-hour journey home, I prayed for the energy to make the long drive alone. About thirty minutes into the journey, we had a flat tire on a deserted stretch of road, and I had no choice but to unload the car on the side of the road in order to access the spare tire.

I didn't know if I wanted to laugh or cry, and in my head, I was thinking, "Seriously, God?!" That was quickly followed by a resigned, "Okay God, give me the strength to deal with this problem and get us home safely."

Despite the less-than-smooth ride home, it remains one of our favorite trips ever. We still laugh every time we look at the picture of our belongings strewn about the grass beside our car with the flat tire!

If you're considering an adventure alone with your kids, don't let the work before, during, and after the activity deter you from going. God will help you find strength for the journey, and even if there are some bumps in the road, He will help you push through. When it's all said and done, it's about the priceless memories made along the way, sometimes even from the side of the road.

Go on the trip! Make precious memories. God will take you where you need to go.

Jesus, please give me strength for the extra work that goes into traveling and exploring new places alone with the kids. Fill us with gratitude for the experiences we share on these adventures and remind us to enjoy the unexpected detours along the way.

PSALM 55:23 · EXODUS 13:21

97 victim to victor

"No, in all these things we conquer overwhelmingly through him who loved us."

— ROMANS 8:37

God has a bold message for you today, my friend: You're not a victim. You're **VICTORIOUS**.

On your hardest days, you may have been knocked down, but you didn't stay down. For the sake of your children, you somehow mustered the energy to climb up, once again, from the mat and continue the fight.

You power through the weariness to care for your children and pay the bills. You smile, sometimes through your own pain and tears, to reassure your children that things will be okay. You show up for your children every day, even on the days when you'd rather crawl under the covers to cry or sleep.

You are a **CHAMPION**.

If you're anything like me, there are definitely days when you feel more like a victim than victorious. It feels too hard to keep going and unfair that you have to face all this alone. It's a battle to get through the day.

Thank goodness this battle belongs to God, not to you or me. God sees you and promises that, through Him, you will not just conquer. You will conquer *overwhelmingly*.

When you find yourself feeling a little less than victorious, it might be time to intentionally generate energy and focus that will help you face the day. Of course, the best place to start is prayer. As you invite God into the process, ask Him to clear your mind of anything that might be bringing you down, to help you prioritize what's most important for today, to fill you with confidence and determination that you can and will face the challenges in your day head-on and without fear.

Then, do your part to stir that spark into a flame of motivation.

For me, that often means listening to my "pre-game" music playlist to get pumped up for the day. One of my favorite songs on that list is "Battle Belongs" by Phil Wickham. This song always reminds me that the battle belongs to God and that through Him I will have victory. Another song on the playlist that immediately stirs up a sense that I am fierce and ready to handle whatever comes my way is the song "The Champion" by Carrie Underwood. (If you haven't heard these songs, give them a listen! You'll feel like you're ready to stand tall and jump in the ring for another round.)

Maybe, today is the day to create your own pre-game music playlist for the times when you need to be uplifted and reminded that you're not a victim—you're victorious. If music isn't your thing, what stirs up a feeling inside you that, through God, you are strong, invincible, and ready to achieve victory? In what way could you incorporate this into your day to set the tone, raise your confidence, and inspire you to persevere?

Jesus, when I am tempted to give into weariness, fear, or despair, remind me that the battle belongs to You. Fill me with bold confidence that, through You, I will overwhelmingly conquer the challenges I face today and that I will be victorious.

JEREMIAH 20:11 · 2 CHRONICLES 20:15

98 **worthy**

"To this end, we always pray for you, that our God may make you worthy of his calling and powerfully bring to fulfillment every good purpose and every effort of faith..."

— 2 THESSALONIANS 1:11

I would be willing to guess that, like me, you often feel unworthy of God's calling for your life, in part because you are single parent. It's tempting to say, "My life is a mess in so many ways. God couldn't possibly be calling me to more."

But, my friend, He IS calling you to more.

Even Peter felt unworthy when Jesus initially called him to be a disciple. Peter's response was, "Depart from me, Lord, for I am a sinful man." Yet, look at what Jesus was able to accomplish through Peter! Jesus made Peter worthy of his calling to lead the apostles, and ultimately, the early Church, and Jesus wants to do similarly amazing things with you. All you have to do is answer the call.

As a single parent, it's easy to make excuses for putting off an answer to God's call, even if you do feel worthy, because it seems like your life should only be about your kids right now. I spent many years thinking, "I'll get to that later when the kids are grown and gone."

What if I told you that your "later" might just be *now* and that you *are* already worthy of the call?

You have sacrificed so much for your kids as any good parent would do, and that is commendable. You pour so much of yourself into your children, but you're also still an individual apart from your role as a parent. You are a person with many gifts, and God is calling you to be a good steward of those gifts.

Go back to Peter's story. He hesitated when Jesus first called him. He denied Jesus three times. He made a lot of mistakes in the Gospels. But in the end, he fully embraced Jesus' call and his legacy is extraordinary. When we embrace God's call, amazing things become possible. All we have to do is respond in faith that He will accomplish great things through us when we respond to His call.

Your life as an individual doesn't resume years down the road when your kids are older, and your worth is not diminished by your single parent status. Your life is NOW, and you are worthy of whatever God is calling you to do.

How is God calling you to be a light to the world right from where you are today? What small step could you take to get the ball rolling on a calling that God has for you beyond your labor of love as a parent?

Jesus, please clearly show me the calling that You have for my life. Remind me that I am worthy of this call and stir into flame my readiness to act on it.

1 PETER 4:10 · MATTHEW 5:14-16

99 prisoners of hope

"Return to a fortress, O prisoners of hope; This very day, I announce I am restoring double to you."

— ZECHARIAH 9:12

My son is one of the most optimistic people I've ever known. At the age of five, he adopted the motto "think good things, and good things happen." And it has served him well! From talking me into giving him an extra cookie for dessert or winning the spelling bee at school, so many outcomes have gone his way. Of course, my son didn't believe that he could manifest these good things all by himself. Rather, he believed that he had a loving Father in Heaven who had good plans for him and would move mountains for him if he did his part to make things happen.

To this day, my son approaches every situation with profound confidence in God to guide the way and meet his needs. No matter the odds, he lives as a "prisoner of hope," and he has inspired me to do the same, especially in those moments when I start to worry that what I've lost will never be restored.

The term "prisoner of hope" is jarring to me every time I read it. It comes from the Book of Zechariah where you and I are called to be prisoners of hope that God will keep His promise of restoration. At times, as a single parent, you might feel more like a prisoner of your past or despair than a prisoner of hope. What's interesting about this kind of prison is that you are both the captive *and* captor. YOU hold the key to your cell. YOU can decide whether to lock yourself in the prison of your past or despair or in a prison of hope.

Have you longed for restoration and wondered when, or even if, it's coming? The longer you wait for restoration, the more tempting it can be to lose hope in God's many promises to restore you. It's easy to fall into the trap of thinking, "If God were going to fix this, He would have done it by now." God's timing is always perfect, but it doesn't always feel that way. (Just ask the Israelites who were wandering in the desert for forty years!)

When you feel like giving up hope, pause to remind yourself why you should remain a prisoner of hope—because God *always* keeps His promises. He hasn't just promised to restore you a little. He's promised to restore double what you lost, and you can count on Him to keep His Word. God is able to "accomplish far more than all we ask or imagine" (Ephesians 3:20). Believe that He sees you, He has not forgotten you, and He has such good plans for you.

In what area(s) of your life are you struggling to remain a prisoner of hope for God's restoration?

Each time that worry pops into your mind today, make a conscious choice to "think good things." Capture that thought and replace it with a profession of your faith in God's love and promises to restore you. Choose to be a prisoner of hope. The more often you consciously replace your doubts with hope, the easier it will be to notice as God makes "good things happen." Restoration is coming, my friend. It's only a matter of time.

Jesus, fill me with unwavering hope in God's promises of restoration and steady trust in His perfect timing. When the worry creeps in, remind me to "think good things" and then watch as He makes "good things happen."

ZEPHANIAH 3:20 · EPHESIANS 3:20-21

100 **your identity**

"For you are a people holy to the LORD, your God; the LORD, your God, has chosen you from all the peoples on the face of the earth to be a people specially his own."

— DEUTERONOMY 14:2

The worldly standards for success, popularity, and beauty sometimes make it difficult to remember who you really are—and *whose* you are. This can be particularly true for teens. I admire my teenage daughter so much for being so comfortable in her own skin and so confident about who she is despite pressure at school and online to be consumed by what is cool and trendy. Daily, I thank Jesus that she has found her identity in Him and is more concerned with figuring out His plan for her life than what the world says she should do and be.

I often wish I could consistently be more like my daughter in this way. Before my divorce, I knew who I was. At least, I thought I did. I was confident and successful according to worldly standards. When I became a single parent and my life was flipped upside down, it was like I lost my identity. I was no longer sure of who I was in this new life that was not what I had imagined for myself. I felt lost.

If you sometimes find yourself feeling a bit lost and unsure of who you are now that you're living this single parent life that is so different from the life you dreamed of, know that you have a loving Father who knew you might need reassurance from time to time, so He clearly defined who you are in His Word.

Here's a reminder of who God says that you are—and *whose* you are:

> Isaiah 43:1 – **You are His.**
> Deuteronomy 14:2 – **You are chosen.**
> 2 Corinthians 5:17 – **You are a new creation in Christ.**
> Galatians 2:20 – **You are loved.**
> Ephesians 2:10 – **You have a purpose that was established before you were born and is still intact.**

Your identity is not who you were in the past, nor mistakes you might have made. Being a single parent isn't your only identity. You are a beautiful soul who is profoundly loved and deeply known by your Father in Heaven. Your identity is in Christ and in who He is calling you to be. Yes, even now. Jesus loves you unconditionally, so much so that He died to save you. Let go of worldly standards and know your incredible worth in His eyes. THAT is who you are, and with Jesus by your side, the best is yet to come!

Jesus, my Lord and my life, fill me with the peace and self-worth that can only come from knowing my identity is in You. Release me from any lingering feelings of shame or grief tied to my past, so I can be free to focus on You and who You're calling me to be.

EPHESIANS 2:10 · 2 CORINTHIANS 5:17

101 **reaping the rewards**

"The God of all grace who called you to his eternal glory through Christ Jesus will himself restore, confirm, strengthen, and establish you after you have suffered a little."

— 1 PETER 5:10

Parenting by yourself is hard.
Trying to constantly figure out how to make ends meet is hard.
Feeling lonely and isolated is hard.
Being so weary that you're not sure you can keep going is hard.
Taking care of your home by yourself is hard.

Without a doubt, God is asking you to do hard things right now.
But He is going to richly reward you.

Through this struggle, God will restore and renew you.
And, if you continue to turn to Him, He'll use this to solidify a firm faith in your heart that can't be shaken.

Keep going.
One day, you will see the fruits of your labor and reap the harvest.
And so will your children.

Jesus, right now, the work of parenting is so heavy and so hard that, some days, I'm worried I'm not going to make it. Please help me hold on and keep going to the finish line so my children and I can reap the rewards that I know You will bring to us through this experience.

GALATIANS 6:9 · 2 CORINTHIANS 4:16

KELLY LUGO is an author, speaker, project manager, single mom, and wrangler of *all* the things. She has two children and more than sixteen years of experience as a single parent. Kelly resides in Texas and is fueled by God's love, her faith, a deep sense of purpose—and lots of coffee. Her mission is sparking hope and healing for other single parents by sharing Biblical wisdom and personal insights about God's promises of providence, protection, and peace. Learn more about inviting Kelly to speak at your church or single parent events or simply reach out to connect with Kelly at **KELLYLUGO.com**.